Power of the Mind

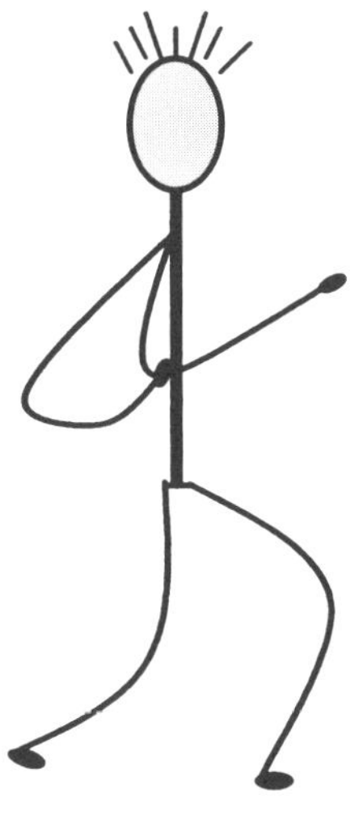

I am delighted that Raman is at last sharing his lifelong wisdom for the benefit of all. *Power of the Mind* is a ***must read*** for anyone who wants to transform one's life, and tap into the incredible power that exists within each of us. I absolutely recommend this book and Raman's *Power of the Mind* Workshops.

— **C.P. GURNANI**
President, Tech Mahindra Ltd

I can confidently attest that the *Power of the Mind* book and Workshops are a reflection of Raman's life experience and learning. I have personally gained tremendously from the ideas and practical techniques offered in the *Power of the Mind*, and highly recommend it to anyone interested in personal growth.

— **Dr. GHASSAN Y. YACOUB**
Founder of IndiaWorld

Power of the Mind provides leaders with a straightforward method to fully harness the creativity, productivity, energy and power of the mind to radically transform themselves and their organizations.

— **Dr. JACQUELINE LOPEZ**
Organizational Development, Intel

Power of the Mind captures Raman's secrets for health, well-being and personal success in an easy to read format. I have personally benefited from Raman's teachings and strongly believe ***this book will change your life***!

— **JOHN B. HANSEN**
Software Engineering Manager

Takes the mystery out of meditation and yoga, provocative juicing recipes for good dieting and high energy, and makes marathoning a possibility for anyone. In all, an everyday life tool for self care towards wellness.

— **GRACE HUI**
Women's Health Nurse Practitioner,
Certified Legal Nurse Consultant

I wish every parent could read *Power of the Mind*. It isn't just for corporate executives! As a busy mom, I appreciate that this book is simple and concise. I could grasp the concepts immediately and I now feel confident that I am ready to begin my own path to personal fulfillment.

— **KATHRYN AXTELL**
Mother of three,
Assistant Scoutmaster and Professional Volunteer

For over 25 years that I have known Raman, he has been an amazing role model for self-discipline and single mindedness of purpose. In *Power of the Mind*, Raman has shared the cornerstones of his personal success in a sincere, straight-forward and lucid manner. *Power of the Mind* offers a no-nonsense, no frills formula that can be put into practice to achieve optimal health and meet your personal and professional goals.

— **JASJIT KAUR**
Co-Founder, International Institute of Gurmat Studies

Power of the Mind

Experiencing, Harnessing and Utilizing the Force Within

Raman

Star Galaxy Publishing

Published by:
Star Galaxy Publishing
1058 Treeline Drive
Allentown, PA 18103
Phone: 888-727-7296, Fax: 610-391-7296
http://www.stargalaxypub.com

WARNING - DISCLAIMER

The recommendations in this book are based on personal experience of the author. Because each person and situation is unique, the publisher urges the reader to check with a qualified health professional before following any recommendation. The author and publisher are not responsible for any adverse consequences resulting from the use of any suggestions or preparations in this book. If in doubt about anything, please consult a physician or other qualified health professional before proceeding. The author and the publisher make no warranty of any kind, expressed or implied, with regard to material contained in this book, all of which is provided "as is". The author and the publisher shall not be liable for any direct or indirect damages arising from any use, direct or indirect, of the information provided in this book.

Printed in Canada

10 9 8 7 6 5 4 3 2 1

Library of Congress Control Number: 2006925961

ISBN-13: 978-0-9650391-4-7
ISBN-10: 0-9650391-4-5

To my parents and maternal uncles (Masarji and Mamaji) who started me on my journey in meditation and exploring the power of the mind.

Deep within man dwell those slumbering powers; powers that would astonish him, that he never dreamed of possessing; forces that would revolutionize his life if aroused and put into action.

— Orison S. Marden

Table of Contents

List of Illustrations

Preface

The books that have been written on the subject of meditation, yoga, and the power of positive thinking are too numerous to list here. What, then, prompted me to act like there was anything new to add to the volumes that already existed in bookstores everywhere?

I believe I have a different perspective on the subject, based on nearly 35 years experience of practicing and teaching the subject, while continuing to work in the corporate world. My BSEE/MBA and 28 years in the high-tech industry make me an unlikely candidate for teaching, much less writing a book, about Mind Power. Yet, it is this very background that makes my program believable.

Like many people, I have a day job with a family and three children. In my "spare" time, I still find time to be a Scoutmaster in my community, run marathons, and teach workshops on *Power of the Mind.* The reason is that I have found a way to incorporate all these into my life without inducing stress. The *Power of the Mind* talks about the simple changes that can be made in one's life, to get the most out of it.

My first exposure to meditation was at the tender age of twelve. Thirty-eight years later, I can say it was the best thing that ever happened to me.

Being of a scientific bent of mind, one might ask what caused me to lean towards something as abstract as meditation at that early age. It was more an act of desperation than something planned and thought through.

I was a chubby kid in school and needled by my classmates. Many of them called me football, instead of by my given name. I went through a lot of anguish and resentment. Sensing my anger and frustration one day, my mother told me that getting upset was harming no one but myself. Instead, she asked me to sit down quietly, close my eyes, and "see" people accepting, and even applauding, me.

At first, I was unable to frame that picture in my mind. Over time, I found I could go into my hidden sanctuary at will. It helped me relax and become more secure within myself. Two additional changes occurred. First, my classmates stopped making fun of me since it no longer evoked a reaction. Second, I started seeing myself as a healthy and athletic boy in my mind. I started on a jogging program — not the easiest task for me. Over the course of a year, I was looking in real life the way I had pictured myself in my mind's eye.

Growing in a household with a family history of diabetes and heart disease, it was easy to attribute everything to heredity. It provided me with a ready excuse for my excessive weight, my desire for sweets — after all, it was all in my genes. However, my experience with meditation and the glimpse I had of what my mind could do with my weight control problem convinced me that I had only scratched the surface. Having seen the ravages caused by acute diabetes at close quarters, I decided I wanted no part of it.

Drawing on my scientific and engineering background, coupled with 35 years of experience in meditation, I developed a program that has enabled me to stay stress-free and healthy, eliminate back pain, and get younger with each passing day over the past 15 years. I have greater endurance, strength and flexibility than I had in my twenties.

I wrote the *Power of the Mind* to help individuals experience the energy source within, tap into their energy source, and utilize it to enrich their lives in a multitude of ways. The information in this text is based on personal experience and the feedback from participants who have practiced the principles taught at the *Power of the Mind* workshops (see http://www.power-of-the-mind.com). This book is meant to reach out to those unable to attend the workshops, but who would like to enjoy a rich and rewarding life.

Acknowledgments

I want to thank everyone who has asked a question about *Power of the Mind*, prompting me to find answers for them. Special thanks to Gordon Chinn, CP Gurnani, John Hansen, Ghassan Yacoub, and all the people who attended the *Power of the Mind* workshops/retreats over the years, and provided affirmation that the principles outlined in this book worked for each of them.

I would like to reiterate my thanks to everyone who took time to review this book and make invaluable suggestions. I would especially like to acknowledge Jacqueline Lopez and J. Bhasker for reviewing the manuscript at various stages and for all of their helpful suggestions and insight.

For their honest feedback and help in coming up with the final book cover design, my grateful thanks to my family.

Finally, I would like to thank my wife, Roma, for painstakingly going through the final manuscript in detail.

— *Raman*

Foreword

Greetings and Salutations! My name is Gordon and I am a senior manager at a major technology company. Your first reaction is probably, "Who is this guy and why is he writing a foreword for a *mind-power* kind of book?". It is true that I am not a published author of any "self-improvement" books or classes, but I have been a "seeker" of self-improvement for over twenty-five years and have tried numerous mental and physical improvement programs and therefore, feel at least qualified to give a first-hand testimony for the *Power of the Mind* program. In any case, please bear with me for another page or two and hopefully, my experiences will be of interest to you, but if you're anxious to get to the "good stuff", feel free to just skip this section and jump right in. Suffice to say then that the techniques and concepts introduced in this book and classes have altered my life and well-being in quantum leaps that no other program has done so in the past and I firmly believe that you too can reap these wonderful and seemingly "miraculous" benefits.

To use the phrase, "self-improvement" is precarious in that it is not only an overly used phrase like, "Thinking out of the box" or "You can do it!", but it can also conjure up pre-conceived images of infomercials, quick-results scams, negative experiences from such programs, or reactions of "Been there, done that" or "I don't need it" or "Too airy/fairy for me". I have to admit that I have been guilty of all above examples. On the other hand, there is always some level of risk-taking (or leap of faith) when undertaking something new and there is always some level of effort required, even if it's only to pick up the phone and give out your credit card number. Regarding *Power of the Mind,* however, I can personally attest that it is well worth your time to try it with very little downside and significant upside.

The goal of the *Power of the Mind* program is to assist one in attaining holistic well-being or a state of being where the body and mind function as one. How one attains this state of well-being is described in the four cornerstones: meditation, yoga, diet, and exercise. Many books have been written on these topics, especially on diet and exercise and many people, including myself, have tried various programs with varying levels of success, but more frequently than not, initial enthusiasm eventually ends up in failure to sustain a program. An often cited example is the New Year's resolution of losing excess weight where most people eventually give up and go back to their original unhealthy life habits.

Why does this happen and how then does one break this destructive "ping-pong" cycle? Based on personal experience, I believe this happens because the mind/body is not working as "one". In my case, I was running six miles a day and I was in top physical form. Eventually, however, I became "burnt out" and gave up running for over ten years. I now realize that I gave up because I was exercising for the wrong reason which was to "look physically fit" instead of doing what was "right" for me. What I learned in this program was that when I know what was "right" for me (the mental part), I will naturally do the right physical (diet/exercise/yoga) things (the body part). All this happens simply and naturally, without any internal struggles, without guilt, and without the need to have "will-power". When my mind/body is operating as one, I naturally do the right things.

So how does one determine what is "right"? It turns out that meditation is the key cornerstone to be absolutely clear of what is "right" for you. When one clearly knows what is "right", inner peace is attained which is the basis for all other mental and physical benefits to follow. In other words, the mind and body are now working as one, naturally and of its own volition. The right things "just happen".

Does this all really work? I can only speak from personal experience and similar comments from my colleagues. The *Power of the Mind* program has improved the quality of my life in quantum leaps when compared against other single-focused programs that I have tried in the past. After attending the 3-day *Power-of-the-Mind* (PoM) seminar over seven months ago, the quality of my work and personal life continues to improve dramatically: physically, mentally, and spiritually. While initially motivated by the stresses of working in a fast-pace technology field, the benefits of practicing the principles of PoM has crossed over into my personal life. Many companies espouse the importance of work-life balance, but few that I know of, actually provide the tools to achieve this elusive goal. I am very fortunate to work for a company that has given me these tools, through PoM. I would like to describe a few areas where my life has changed.

First, my overall stress level has been reduced dramatically, even though my work and personal life demands have not changed, as contradictory as this may sound. In some cases, the demands have increased. Throughout the seminar, we are reminded that "it's all in your mind". While sounding all too simplistic and trendy, my belief in this concept has grown daily, not by simple faith, but by personal experiences that forms the basis of my belief. By practicing the techniques learned in the PoM, I was taught to quiet the mind from all of the hundreds, if not thousands of thoughts, positive and negative, that stream continuously though my mind daily. By quieting and calming my mind, I am now able to focus on the most important issues and actions that need to be taken at any one time. Since my stress level is determined by the number of demands (perceived or real), my stress levels have dramatically reduced because I only need to focus on a few items at any one moment. Everything else is of lower urgency or importance so I do not have to spend mental energy on them or at least, defer them to a later time. While all this sounded very logical and reasonable and I had probably read all of this in various self-improvement magazine articles, actually making it happen was difficult. Practicing the simple techniques taught in PoM, however, put all of the missing pieces together and allowed the principles to be effective. Having lower stress levels, however, does not end there. My business (and personal) relationships have improved dramatically, resulting in higher team productivity, higher levels of collaboration between teams from different cultures and countries, and higher levels of employee satisfaction and passion (fun). All this was part of our company's goal for stress reduction as well to enable "transformational" leadership of projects and people. The fact is that transformation leadership in a corporation starts with personal transformation, not the other way around. I know this concept may sound far-fetched, but based on multiple personal experiences that go beyond simple luck and coincidence, I firmly believe this is true.

Second, my energy levels have dramatically increased. While previously needing a minimum of 8 hours of sleep daily, I now only need 4-5 hours on the average. In other words, I need less than 4 hours when needed or desired and more than 4 hours if needed or desired. Furthermore, jet lag is no longer a major problem; I can step off a plane after passing through many time zones and feel energetic and able to focus on the task at hand. I cannot explain it, but it seems as if my focus is no longer ensuring that I have enough sleep, but rather, the focus is now living life contentedly and sleeping when my body tells me it's time. It reminds me a little of my young son, experiencing life moment to moment, and when he needs sleep, he sleeps, sometimes for only a few minutes and sometimes for many hours. Also, after giving up jogging for over ten years, I have resumed my jogging program during the past three months with plans to run a marathon in a few months. My training program has been almost "effortless", being able to add a mile each week without stress or injuries. The key difference between now and running 6 miles a day ten years ago is that I am now jogging for the right reason and listening to (the mind part) and then doing what's best for my body which is the result of having my mind and body operating as one. The result is that I'm jogging further than before and enjoying it more. The focus is on doing what's "really" right for me and not on what others want me to do or what I think others will think of me. Finally, even previous food allergies have mostly disappeared — can't explain it, but I am beginning to expect these "miracles".

Third, my overall quality of life is much higher. Little things that previously caused anger, disappointment, or fear do not occur as often. For example, my long drive to work through heavy traffic used to irritate me greatly, especially when "someone does something stupid", like cutting in front of me or going slow in the fast lane. At some times, I seem to just "sail" through heavy traffic. While busier than ever, I no longer need to rush as much. Life quality in the past was largely determined by the number of tasks completed or meeting certain high standards. I no longer try to cram as much into my life as possible. It's more than the old phrase of "more quality, less quantity" or "smelling the roses". With more calmness and requiring less sleep, I've actually achieved both higher quality and quantity and more importantly, higher contentment. I no longer worry much now; they are just fleeting thoughts that come and go. In the past, I used to "worry" about almost everything: job success, personal health, family happiness, getting old, financial security, etc. Now, I focus on what's right for me moment-by-moment which allows me to calmly and effectively handle all of the issues that are really important. Interestingly, I do not need to consciously be "one with the universe", or be "in-tune" with myself; life just seems to flow more effortlessly. In other words, "life is good" was always good (as Raman would gently remind us), and the future is now filled with endless opportunities (no cliché intended).

If you've actually read down to this point, hopefully something I've described has caught your interest. On the other hand, perhaps you feel that it was just another infomercial ..... "It sounds too good to be true". In both cases, go with your "gut"; it's your inner voice telling you that you are ready for a "refresh" in your life. I highly recommend the *Power of the Mind* program and encourage you to "check it out". Based on my experiences, I firmly believe you too will experience wonderful benefits when you are "one in mind and body".

Section I

Principles of Wellbeing

Chapter 1

An Introduction to Wellness

Most of us realize very early in life that to get the best results in any endeavor, we need to get all the parts working in unison towards a common goal. For instance, a child will have difficulty getting his toy truck up a ramp when a friend is pulling in the opposite direction. Similarly, a soccer team would find it extremely frustrating to win against an opponent, if some of the players kept kicking the ball towards their own goal. While these examples state the obvious, they underscore a very important point, namely the need for alignment to achieve desired results. So it is with our complex human machinery.

Holistic well-being or wellness is the state of being when the body and mind function as an integrated whole. Recognition of the 'oneness' of body and mind is vital to the achievement of perfect health and happiness. There are numerous case studies demonstrating the power of the mind in helping people rapidly recover from serious illnesses. I personally know of an individual with sea-food allergies, who would break out at the slightest hint of shell-fish. Today, he can enjoy shell-fish to his heart's content without the slightest trace of illness. Once the mind is convinced of a desired outcome, the body will follow suit.

The same is true of athletic achievements. For example, runners fell short of the 4-minute mile for years. Yet, within months of Roger Bannister breaking the 4-minute barrier, the feat was repeated multiple times. Once it was internalized that the task could be accomplished, a host of athletes discovered they had the physical prowess to do it. The mind can indeed be a very powerful ally.

In all instances in this text, the mind refers to the "inner mind" as differentiated from the intellect or rational mind. This is an important distinction, as there are pitfalls associated with undue reliance on the rational mind. For instance, I can choose not to exercise and blame my obesity on genetics. Or I could sit in front of the television each evening and rationalize that I do so since there are no activities in the neighborhood. The intellect can be used to justify and provide excuses for personal failures.

It is also the intellect that limits one to accepting only what is the norm. For instance, if the current medical literature on the subject states that a bout of influenza will last a week, or a sprained back needs weeks to recover, we make it a self-fulfilling prophecy by internalizing the information and generating the will to make it come true. On the other hand, one can get in touch with the inner-mind and tap into the limitless energy resources to recover rapidly, if one succumbs to ailments in the first place. This is covered in greater detail in subsequent chapters in this book.

More and more thought is being given today to the effect of our emotions on the physical self. Given this heightened awareness, how does one get the mind and body to function as an integrated unit? The answer is that they actually do function as one — we just don't recognize it in our daily lives. So, what really needs to happen is to increase one's awareness of the self — to come alive and benefit from holistic health and well-being.

To be fully alive, one has to be:

1. Physically fit

2. Mentally active

3. Emotionally secure

4. Spiritually aware

These four aspects of wellness are not separable, but an integral part of your being. If one part is not well, the whole cannot be well. It is imperative that all four be in harmony and balance to attain perfect health and well-being.

Most literature on the subject tends to focus on either the physical (through exercise), or the mental/ emotional (through psychology). And spirituality is often associated with religion. This text attempts to steer clear of the stereotypes, and describe a lifestyle that will focus on all four aspects of well-being, including a step-by-step guide on how to achieve complete well-being.

Last, but not least, Appendix A introduces the subject of Ayurveda, which offers an alternate perspective of well-being. For a more detailed exposition on the subject, the reader can refer to the myriads of books on the subject available in most public libraries.

THOUGHT FOR THE DAY

YOU OWE IT TO YOURSELF TO BE FULLY ALIVE!

Chapter 2

Cornerstones of Holistic Health

There are four cornerstones that form the basis of holistic health — Meditation, Yoga/Stretching, Exercise and Diet (Figure 1). Each contributes to one or more of the four aspects of well-being — Physical, Mental, Emotional and Spiritual as described in the preceding chapter.

Each cornerstone has an effect on different aspects of our well-being. Each helps sustain the others and build them in an upward spiral towards perfect health and well-being.

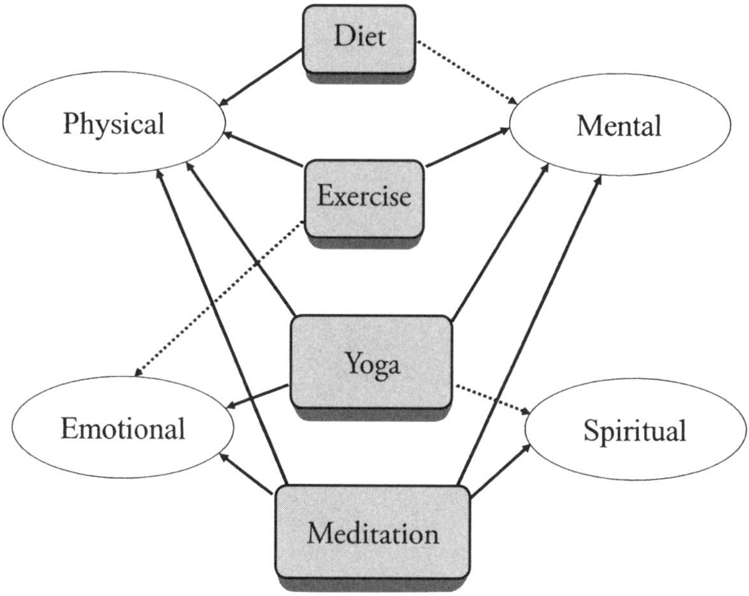

Figure 1 *Cornerstones of Holistic Health.*

Diet

Diet has a direct impact on physical well-being. As the saying goes, we are what we eat. We are all aware of the ill-effects of indulging in high-fat or sodium-rich foods. Current research also shows a correlation between certain kinds of foods and our state of mind. For example, we are more likely to be irritated if our blood-sugar runs low. Yet, for all the focus on diet, its impact is diluted and rendered insignificant in the absence of the other cornerstones.

Exercise

Exercise affects our physical and mental well-being. Just a 20-minute jog performed consistently thrice weekly transforms our bodies into high-energy reservoirs. Exercise has a similar effect on our mental state. We have all heard of a runner's high. Endorphins released during exercise help relax the mind. It has an indirect effect on our emotional well-being. However, exercise again contributes only to a small part of our well-being.

Yoga

Most of the forms of yoga have a direct bearing on our physical, mental, and emotional well-being. Yoga helps through increased flexibility, greater relaxation, and a calming of the senses. It can also help spiritual growth tangentially. This is a very important cornerstone that helps you maintain exercise and diet programs, through fewer injuries and a relaxed state of mind.

Meditation

Meditation holds the key to physical, mental, emotional, and spiritual health. It is the basis for all well-being. Through meditation, you can attain complete wellness by unifying every facet of your health.

Yoga, exercise and diet contribute because a healthy body houses a healthy mind.

However, everything starts with meditation. Meditation is a state in which the body is consciously relaxed and the mind is allowed to become calm and focused.

- The calming of the mind results in:
  - The ensuing resolve (from within).
  - The ability to continue a program successfully.
  - The recognition of the physical (body), mental (brain/rational mind), emotional (psyche) and spiritual (inner mind) being ONE entity.

You can strengthen your mind, and resolve, through meditation. Meditate on who you want to be. You have to delve deep into yourself, past the rational mind, and get to the inner mind. You have to believe in yourself. In many cases, it is the fear of failure that leads people to live a sedentary lifestyle and not step out of their comfort zone and do something different. I have talked with many people who have used the "time" excuse for not exercising, because they were afraid that they would fall short of their goals — be it weight loss or completing a race. It's because we constantly strive to live up to other's expectations.

Through meditation, you will reach a state of poise. You will be at peace with yourself. You will recognize that failure exists only in the mind. You can set yourself up for success. Through your inner confidence, you can now embark on a program that leads to your personal growth. You will be cognizant of the following principles:

- Exercising (consistently) is hard => Not exercising is harder (Long-term negative effects).
- Meditation is hard => Not meditating is harder (No peace of mind).
- Eating right is hard => Not eating right is harder (Long-term harmful effects).
- Quitting (drinking/smoking) is hard => Not quitting is harder (Ill Health).

THOUGHT FOR THE DAY

YOU CAN BE COMPLETELY HEALTHY — PHYSICALLY, MENTALLY, EMOTIONALLY AND SPIRITUALLY!

Section II

Power of the Mind

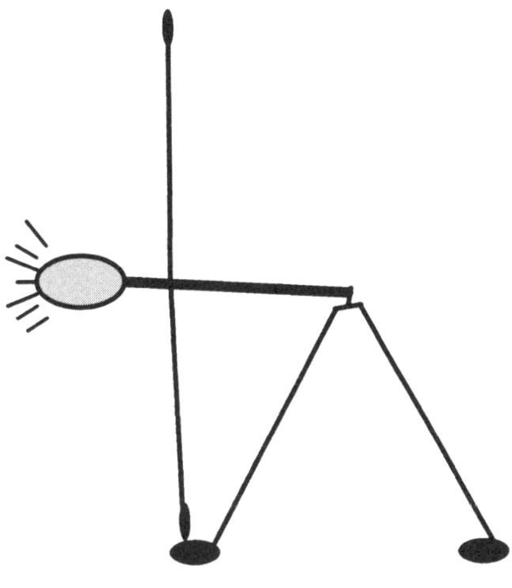

Chapter 3

Experiencing the Power of the Mind

One of the easiest ways to experience the power of the mind is to relax — not try too hard.

- How often have you grappled with a problem, with little success? Once you let go and forget about it, the answer strikes you.

- What about the times you have tried to remember a name, or phone number, or a song? Only to recall it the following day when you no longer have the need.

- Have you ever set the alarm clock for a particular time in the morning, then wake up a couple of minutes before the alarm goes off?

Is this coincidence? Not really! In each case, the desired result is obtained when the mind is not under duress. As soon as the pressure is released, the mind relaxes and begins to function efficiently. Let's take a look at the people who manage to live in this state consistently. Experience the power of the mind vicariously through a family member, friend, or associate. Look around and you will recognize these people. They:

- Are positive
- Generate energy
- Exude confidence

They are alive! They have an aura around them. They can walk into a crowded room and immediately get noticed. People listen when they talk. They are the life of a party.

What makes them special? They have tapped into their minds and are in touch with themselves. This is the inner mind, not the rational mind or brain. In fact, focusing on the intellect is what blocks the natural flow of energy. Just as a boxer rolls with the punches, you want to let the energy flow through you.

Try this simple exercise shown in Figure 2. Wear loose-fitting clothes. Pick a quiet time. Sit down where you are least likely to be disturbed. Close your eyes.

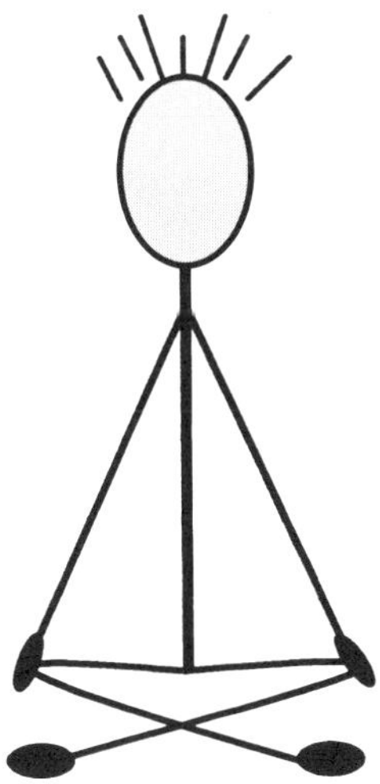

Figure 2 *Meditation Pose.*

Now breathe in slowly — no more than 3-4 breaths per minute. With each breath you take in, feel the life-giving force flow through you to the very depths of your being. As you exhale, feel that energy taking all the tension out of your system. In just a few minutes, you will feel totally relaxed. You will be amazed how long the calming effect of this simple exercise lasts. Now think about what it would be like to draw on that feeling at will. Exhilarating!

THOUGHT FOR THE DAY

TUNE IN TO THE POWER WITHIN YOU!

Chapter 4

Harnessing the Power of the Mind

Many people who have experienced the power of the mind savor it for the moment, revel in it for a while, and then store the memory for the sake of prosperity. They believe it is a random act of nature and are grateful for the experience. What they miss is that this is a glimpse of the power within. There is a whole new world to be explored within your mind. Once you have learned to tune in, you will be able to draw on it as needed to better all aspects of your life.

Just as you would not see an exciting movie preview and then miss the actual screening, so also you should not forego the opportunity to harness this energy after you have had a few random experiences. You trust the movie will be at least as good as the preview. You have to believe your subsequent experiences will be as enriching as the first. And you can experience them each day. I have drawn on this life-giving force within me numerous times over the past quarter of a century.

Harnessing this energy often takes time and patience. This is the chicken-and-egg problem. The people who have the patience are already in a relatively relaxed state of mind and progress faster. The ones who are impatient are the ones that need to tune in to the power, so they can experience the calming effect of the energy. The good news is that no matter what your current state of mind, you can continue to grow and harness the power with each passing day. There is no magic formula. However, here are some methods used to harness this energy.

1. Learn to let go (of your ego).

We believe we control all the events around us. When things don't go as planned, it leads to anger and frustration. This blocks the free flow of energy through our system and impinges on the mind. The next time this happens, notice your breathing becomes heavier as you get upset.

Recognize that life is a learning experience. Sit back and enjoy the play as it unfolds — this does not mean you become disconnected and aloof, but that you do not react to things outside your control. Focus on all the things that have gone your way. Think of those less fortunate than yourself (and pray for them).

As you relax, the breathing becomes easier and the tension melts. You feel calm and are in a state of readiness to experience the power.

2. Meditate daily.

There is an abundance of material available on meditation. I will not go into the details here. I will state that it is sometimes better to have someone work with you when you get started.

Even if it is for a few minutes each morning (or evening), sit down quietly and reflect on the joys of life. Each of us has so much to be grateful for. All the things we take for granted are actually precious gifts — our hands, eyes, ears, house, clothes, and food.

As you give thanks, bring your mind to the energy within you. Relax and feel it flow through your being. Experience the calm and tranquility. Realize that you can draw on this anytime, anywhere. Experience the joy of life.

3. Make Yoga/stretching part of your routine.

A healthy body houses a healthy mind. Through yoga, your body will become both supple and strong. At the very least, you will be able to sit for extended periods of time without fidgeting during meditation.

Additionally, the breathing exercises in yoga can help in relaxation. When performed for extended periods of time, deep breathing can help detoxify the body.

Stretching will keep you limber, and minimize the injuries you might experience in other facets of you life. Stretching offers protection while performing tasks as simple as lifting a heavy object or an extracurricular activity such as jogging.

4. Exercise on a regular basis.

We all know the physical benefits of exercise. But it goes beyond that when you couple it with an outing in nature. Going for a walk in the park or a run in the hills can be therapeutic.

If you tend to keep company when you exercise, steer clear of controversial topics or discussions. Keep in mind that this is part of your relaxation time and take full advantage of it.

5. Have fun!

No matter what the situation, learn to have fun. You may not be able to change the events around you, but you can control how you react to them.

As you go through the cycle of harnessing your power, then utilizing it to stay centered, you will experience a feeling of equipoise and tranquility. Without conscious effort, you will find it emanating from you. You will now become the life of a party; you will exude confidence; you will have that aura around you. But most of all, you will experience the joy of calm contentment.

Thought for the Day

YOU CAN TAP INTO YOUR ENERGY SOURCE!

Chapter 5

Utilizing the Power of the Mind

Utilizing the power of your mind is as easy as drawing water from a well, or turning on the faucet in your kitchen sink. It is like digging a well one time, then utilizing it to water the fields for years to come. The water was always within the ground just waiting to be tapped. Similarly, once you have learned to tune into the power source within you, you can draw from it to grow in all aspects of your life.

I have personally utilized it for:

- Lowering my cholesterol
- Dropping down to my ideal weight
- Alleviating back pain
- Increasing my energy level
- Staying upbeat

The point is that once you are centered, you will have a different perspective on life. You will be calm and collected. You will be secure in the knowledge that you can, and will, succeed at anything you want. Your confidence will manifest itself in the way you respond to situations. No longer will you be the victim, but the master of all you survey.

It's not that the world around you will have changed. It is how you view the world that undergoes a transformation. What you project outside is a reflection of what is within you.

- Remember when you were first in love? You were on cloud nine and nothing could shake you. You may have been penniless with no place to go. But you were happy!
- What about the time when you got your first little pup? He whined and kept you

up all night. Yet you remained unperturbed as a mother with her newborn. Your cup of joy was overflowing!

- On the other hand, when you were mad at having lost a game, or having failed a test, you snapped at everyone around you. You tried to hurt the very people who were trying to help you. It is because you were agitated within.

What is inside you is a microcosm of what manifests itself in the world at large. When you are contented within, you see order in the world. Everything appears to be working according to a plan. When you are disturbed, you project feelings of negativity.

Since the outside world is a mirror reflection of the inner mind, it should come as no surprise that the way to a happier, healthier you, is to stay calm and relaxed. I know there are relaxation tapes given to recovering heart patients after surgery, especially when they exercise. The idea is to enable you to be calm and at peace with yourself.

The mind is like a child at play — constantly running in different directions. It is not normal for the mind to stay at rest. However, with practice, you can learn to bring it back to its center. Over time, it becomes easier to return the mind to its state of equipoise at will. Even if there is turbulence, the trained mind seeks its innate relaxed state quickly.

I have often used personal meditative reflections to ground myself in turbulent times:

- When I am stuck in traffic during rush-hour and start feeling anxious, I make a conscious effort to breathe deeply. I remind myself to be grateful for having a set of wheels under me. I feel grateful that I can transport myself so readily without having to be dependent on another. The result is miraculous! In a matter of moments, I elevate my mental and emotional state to one of well-being and probably ward off high-blood pressure, stress and other maladies.

- When the roof springs a leak, instead of thinking the sky is falling on my head, I remind myself how good it is to have a roof over my head (even a leaking one!). The house shelters me from the elements of nature — heat, cold, or rain. It offers me security and a place to raise my family.

- There is so much to be grateful for. All one has to do is look within, because therein lies the solution. So long as we look externally, there will always be discontent and a feeling of inadequacy. Here are some musings that have helped me center myself. I am grateful for:

    - A healthy body with which to experience and appreciate life.

- These eyes through which I see the beauty around me.
- My arms/hands that enable me to accomplish so many tasks with ease.
- These legs that afford me the opportunity to travel freely (unencumbered).
- The ears to hear joyous sounds with.

✧ Most of all, I am grateful for the opportunity to grow!

THOUGHT FOR THE DAY

UTILIZE YOUR POWER SOURCE AND GROW!

Section III

The Supporting Cornerstones

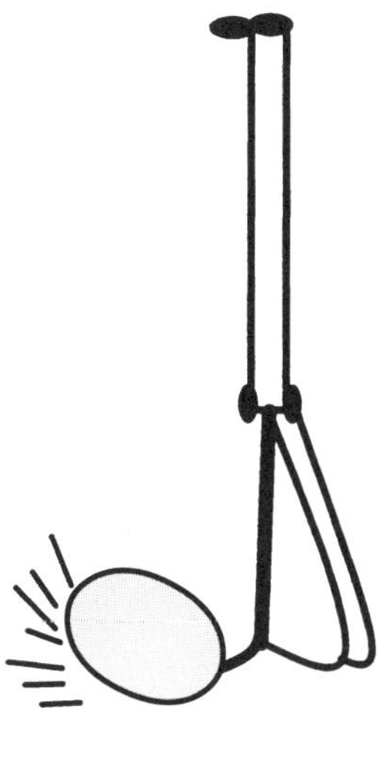

Chapter 6

Yoga

Yoga means different things to different people. There are many branches of Yoga, some leading the student through basic poses; others related to spiritual enlightenment. In this text, we will discuss Yoga in the light of stretching exercises, to supplement the other cornerstones of holistic well-being.

Even within the same branch of Yoga, no two styles of Yoga teach the same pose in the same manner. What follows are a series of exercises, with illustrations, to help you with stretching correctly without injury. If pain is experienced during any of the poses, you are doing too much, or performing the exercise incorrectly. When in doubt, contact an expert on the subject.

Here are a few pointers on getting the most out of your Yoga session.

- Pick a quiet place, where you are least likely to be disturbed.
- Dress in comfortable clothes which don't restrict movement.
- Breathe slowly and easily.
- Keep your mind clear of negative thoughts.
- Always finish your session in the "relaxation" position (see Figure 22).

Mountain Pose

This is the most basic of all exercises and provides the foundation for balance and control of the body. The pose is shown in Figure 3.

1. Start with your feet together, hands at your side, with the eyes looking straight ahead. The heel, toe, and ball of each foot are flat against the floor (see Figure 4A).

2. Pushing into the ground, raise yourself on your toes, stretching the calves and thighs (see Figure 4B).

3. Inhale as you raise your legs.

Figure 3 *Mountain Pose.*

4. Hold the position and your breath for 5-10 seconds.

5. Return to the original standing position as you exhale.

6. The next time you inhale, raise your arms over your head, stretching upwards with your hands and fingers (see Figure 4C, D, & E).

7. Hold the position for 5-10 seconds.

8. Exhale and return to the starting position.

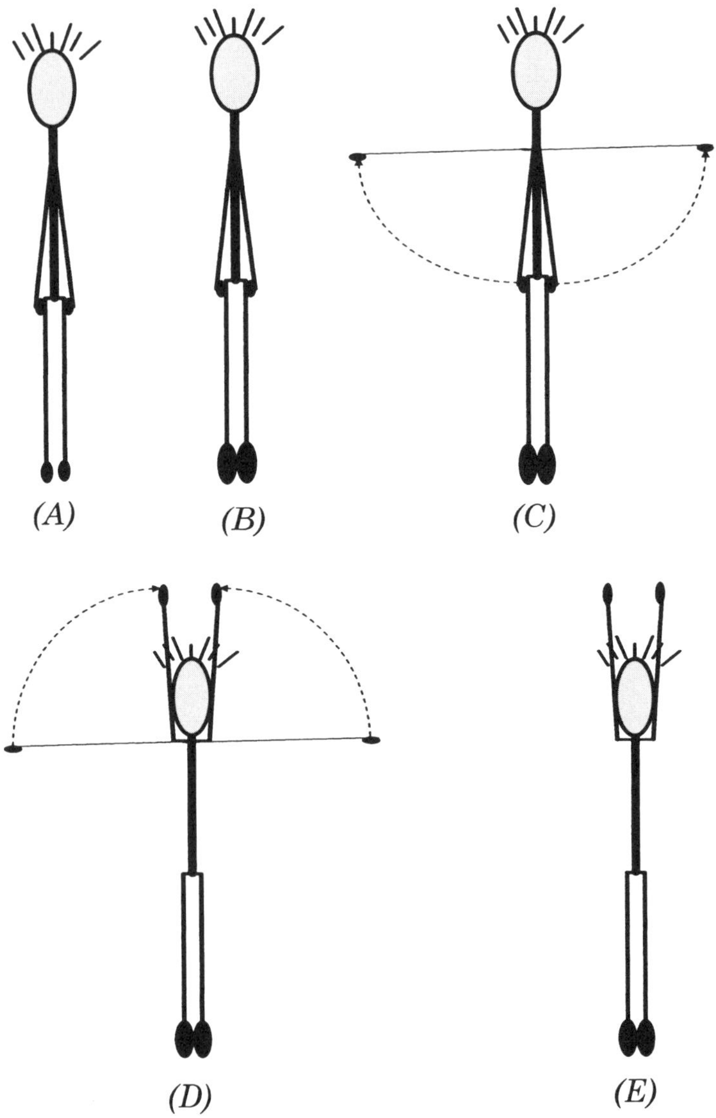

Figure 4 *Steps in Mountain Pose.*

9. Practice raising your arms and legs with each inhalation, and lowering as you exhale.

This is a basic posture of balance and control. It is the foundation for good standing posture.

Forward Bend

All head-below-the-heart Yoga exercises reduce blood pressure. The Forward Bend works the back, hamstring, and abdominal muscles. This is shown in Figure 5.

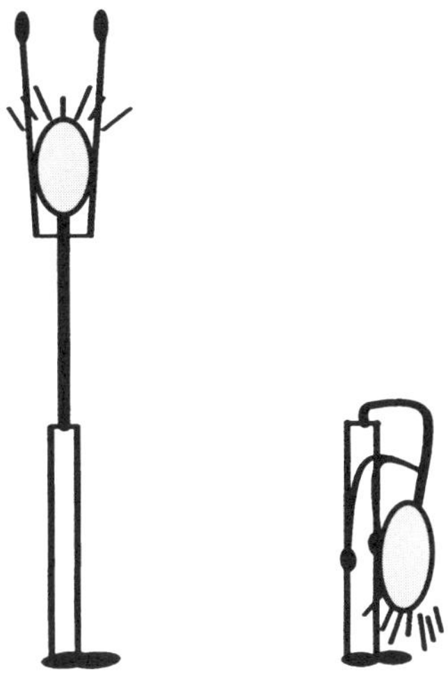

Figure 5 *Forward Bend.*

This exercise should be performed in 3 stages:

First Stage

1. Stand straight, with your hands by your side (see Figure 6A).

2. Raise your arms in front of you, then continue to raise them overhead, bending slightly backward. Inhale throughout this motion (see Figure 6B and Figure 6C).

3. Bend forward from your waist, keeping your arms straight and elbows by your head (see Figure 7A).

4. Keep bending till your head is pointing downwards, and your face is in front of your knees (see Figure 7B & C). Exhale as you bend forward.

5. Grab your knees and hold the stretch for 7 seconds (see Figure 7D). Breathe normally.

6. Pull your body forward to your knees with your hands. Hold for an additional 5 seconds.

7. Slowly uncoil your body and return to the position with arms overhead. Inhale as you raise your body.

8. Bring your arms to your sides.

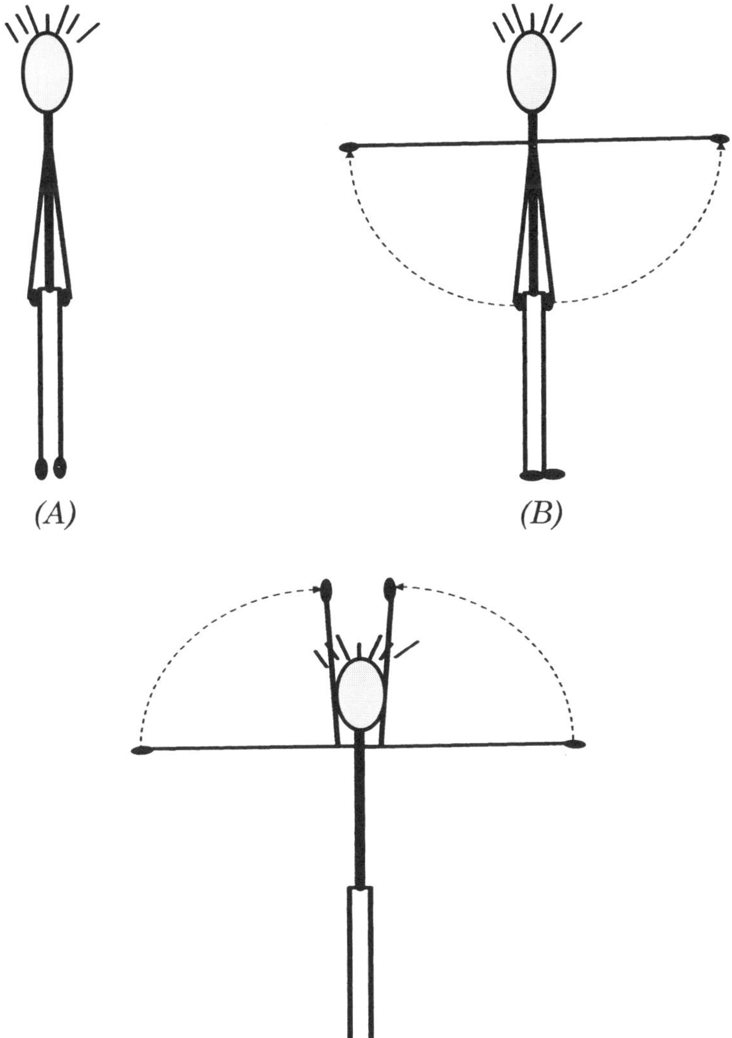

Figure 6 *Steps in Forward Bend.*

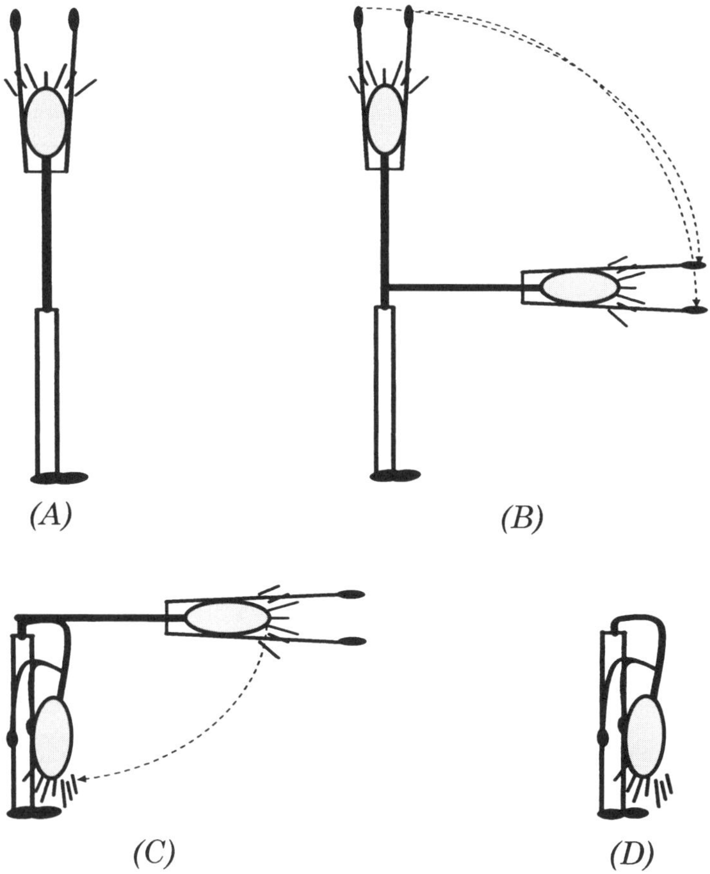

Figure 7 *More Steps in Forward Bend.*

Second Stage

Repeat the exercise with one variation. In steps 5 and 6, you grab your calves with your hands while increasing the stretch.

1. Start in the same position as Stage 1 — standing straight, with your hands by your side.

2. Raise your arms in front of you, then continue to raise them overhead, bending slightly backward. Inhale throughout this motion.

3. Bend forward from your waist, keeping your arms straight and elbows by your head.

4. Keep bending till your head is pointing downwards, and your face is in front of your knees. Exhale as you bend forward.

5. Grab your calves and hold the stretch for 10 seconds. Breathe normally.

6. Pull your body forward to your knees with your hands. Hold for an additional 5 seconds.

7. Slowly uncoil your body and return to the position with arms overhead. Inhale as you raise your body.

8. Bring your arms to your sides.

Third Stage

Repeat the exercise, bending forward a little more. In steps 5 and 6, you grab your ankles with your hands while increasing the stretch.

1. Once again, start in the upright position — standing straight, with your hands by your side.

2. Raise your arms in front of you, then continue to raise them overhead, bending slightly backward. Inhale throughout this motion.

3. Bend forward from your waist, keeping your arms straight and elbows by your head.

4. Keep bending till your head is pointing downwards, and your face is in front of your knees. Exhale as you bend forward.

5. Grab your ankles and hold the stretch for 10 seconds. Breathe normally.

6. Pull your body forward to your knees with your hands. Hold for an additional 5 seconds.

7. Slowly uncoil your body and return to the position with arms overhead. Inhale as you raise your body.

8. Bring your arms to your sides.

Benefits

The Forward Bend alleviates blood pressure and stress. It also tones the abdominal organs, while massaging the liver. Finally, it stretches the hamstring and improves flexibility.

Triangle Pose

Even though this exercise is generally performed in one stage, I prefer to break it into three stages, with the third part forming the Triangular pose (shown in Figure 8). This allows for more gradual stretching for the beginner than if it is performed in a single step.

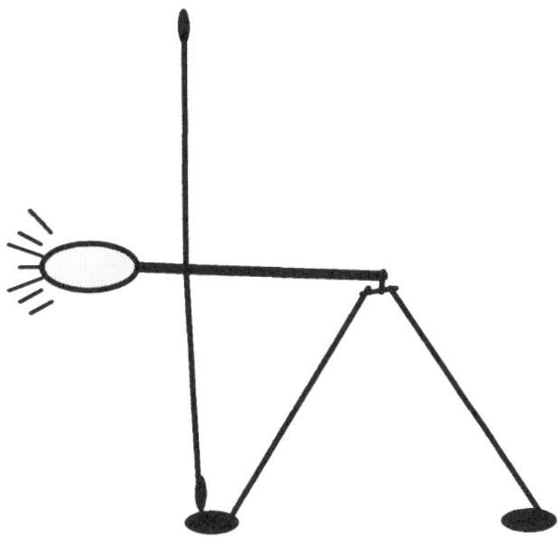

Figure 8 *Triangle Pose.*

First Stage

1. Stand straight, facing forward, with feet about shoulder width apart.

2. Raise your arms shoulder height, palms facing the floor (see Figure 9A).

3. Bring your right hand down to your right knee, with the left hand straight above (see Figure 9B). Exhale when going down.

4. Hold the pose for 7-10 seconds and breathe slowly.

5. Return to the starting position with arms at shoulder height.

6. Repeat with left hand to left knee, and right hand straight above (see Figure 9C & D).

Second Stage

1. Repeat the above exercise with feet 3 feet apart.

2. Raise your arms shoulder height, palms facing the floor.

3. Bring your right hand down to your right calf, with the left hand straight above. Exhale when going down.

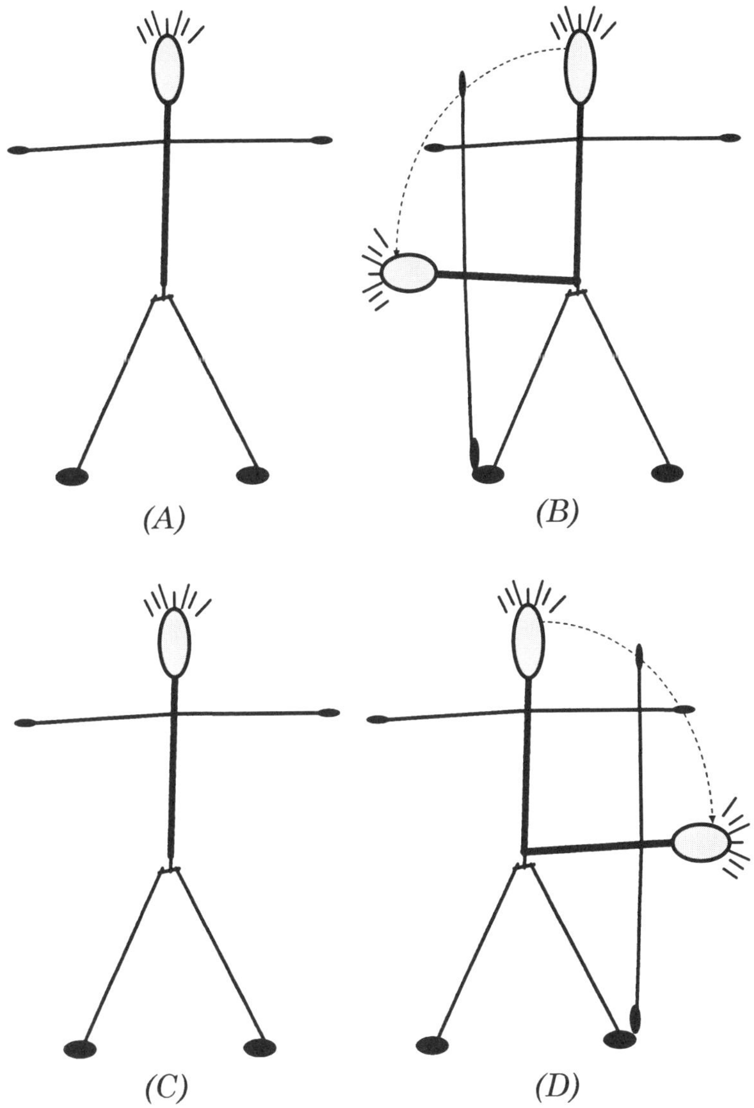

Figure 9 *Steps in Triangle Pose.*

4. Hold the pose for 10-12 seconds and breathe slowly.

5. Return to the starting position with arms at shoulder height.

6. Repeat with left hand to left calf, and right hand straight above.

Third Stage

1. In this final pose, repeat the exercise with feet approximately 4 feet apart.

2. Raise your arms shoulder height, palms facing the floor.

3. Bring your right hand down to your right foot, with the left hand straight above. Exhale when going down.

4. Hold the pose for 12-15 seconds and breathe slowly.

5. Return to the starting position with arms at shoulder height.

6. Repeat with left hand to left foot, and right hand straight above.

In each case, turn the foot towards which the hand is pointing outwards, and the other foot inwards. For example, when the right hand is going down, move the right foot out at an angle of 90 degrees, and the left foot inwards at an angle of 45 degrees. Exhale when moving the arm down towards the leg, and inhale when returning to the starting position with arms at shoulder height.

Benefits

This trims the waistline, and relieves tension in the back and neck. This pose tones leg muscles and helps removes any stiffness in the legs. It also corrects minor deformity in the legs and allows them to develop evenly.

Back Stretch

As the name implies, this increases flexibility of the spine and strengthens the back. It is generally done in four stages. Figure 10 shows this pose.

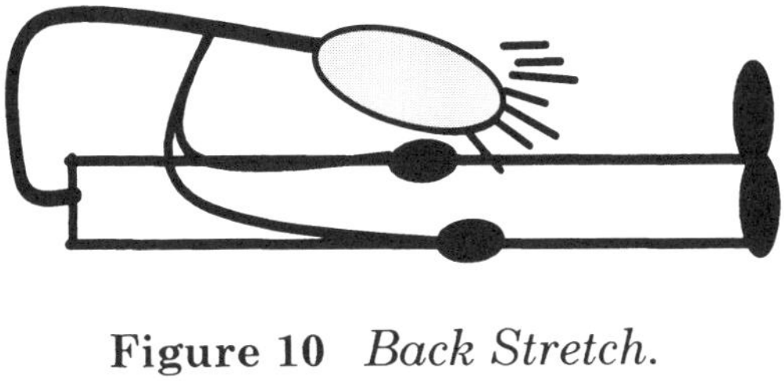

Figure 10 *Back Stretch.*

First Stage

1. Sit on the ground, with legs straight ahead of you.

2. Place your hands on your thighs and straighten your spine (see Figure 11A).

3. Raise your arms in front of you, then continue to raise them overhead, bending slightly backward (see Figure 11B and Figure 11C). Inhale throughout this motion.

4. Bend forward from your waist, exhaling as you go forward (see Figure 11D and Figure 11E).

5. Grab your knees and hold the stretch for 10 seconds. Breathe normally.

6. Pull your body forward to your knees with your hands. Hold for an additional 5 seconds.

7. Slowly uncoil your body and return to the position with arms overhead. Inhale as you raise your body.

8. Return to the starting position.

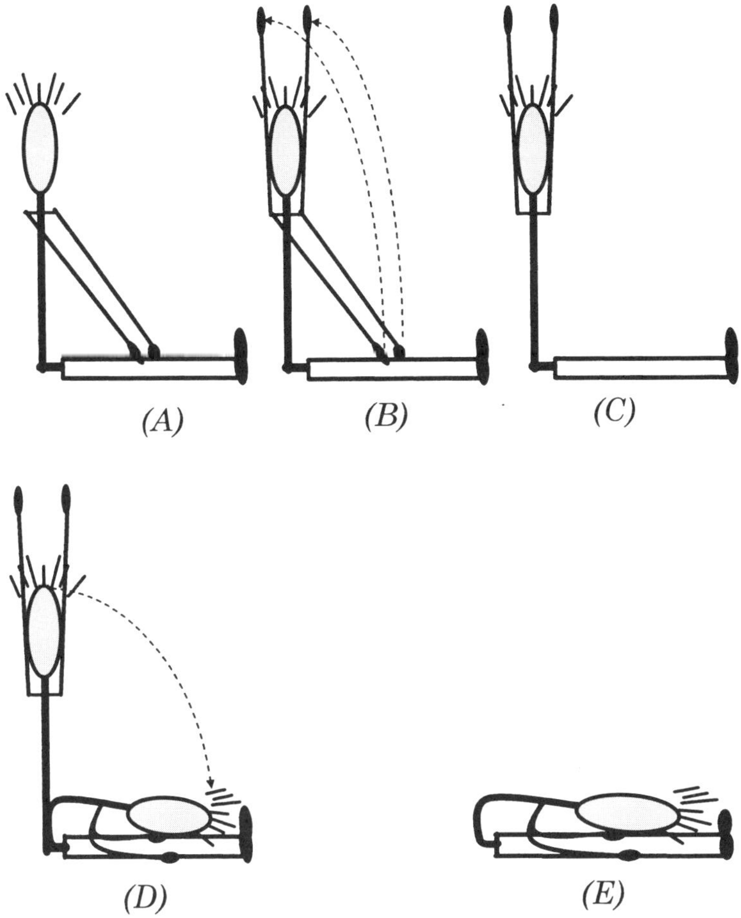

Figure 11 *Steps in Back Stretch.*

Second Stage

Repeat the exercise with one variation. In steps 5 and 6, you grab your calves with your hands while increasing the stretch.

1. Sit on the ground, with legs straight ahead of you.

2. Place your hands on your thighs and straighten your spine.

3. Raise your arms in front of you, then continue to raise them overhead, bending slightly backward. Inhale throughout this motion.

4. Bend forward from your waist, exhaling as you go forward.

5. Grab your calves and hold the stretch for 10 seconds. Breathe normally.

6. Pull your body forward to your knees with your hands. Hold for an additional 5 seconds.

7. Slowly uncoil your body and return to the position with arms overhead. Inhale as you raise your body.

8. Return to the starting position.

Third Stage

Repeat the exercise, bending forward a little more. In steps 5 and 6, you grab your ankles with your hands while increasing the stretch.

1. Sit on the ground, with legs straight ahead of you.

2. Place your hands on your thighs and straighten your spine.

3. Raise your arms in front of you, then continue to raise them overhead, bending slightly backward. Inhale throughout this motion.

4. Bend forward from your waist, exhaling as you go forward.

5. Grab your ankles and hold the stretch for 10 seconds. Breathe normally.

6. Pull your body forward to your knees with your hands. Hold for an additional 5 seconds.

7. Slowly uncoil your body and return to the position with arms overhead. Inhale as you raise your body.

8. Return to the starting position.

Fourth Stage

Repeat the exercise, bending forward a little more. In steps 5 and 6, you grab your toes with your hands while increasing the stretch.

1. Sit on the ground, with legs straight ahead of you.

2. Place your hands on your thighs and straighten your spine.

3. Raise your arms in front of you, then continue to raise them overhead, bending slightly backward. Inhale throughout this motion.

4. Bend forward from your waist, exhaling as you go forward.

5. Reach forward and grab your toes. Hold the stretch for 10 seconds. Breathe normally.

6. Pull your body forward to your knees with your hands. Hold for an additional 5 seconds.

7. Slowly uncoil your body and return to the position with arms overhead. Inhale as you raise your body.

8. Return to the starting position.

Benefits

This increases spinal flexibility and strengthens the back.

Cobra Pose

This exercise gets its name from the way a snake uncoils and gets ready to strike. You need to use your back muscles to raise your chest and upper body off the floor slowly, one vertebra at a time. This pose is shown in Figure 12.

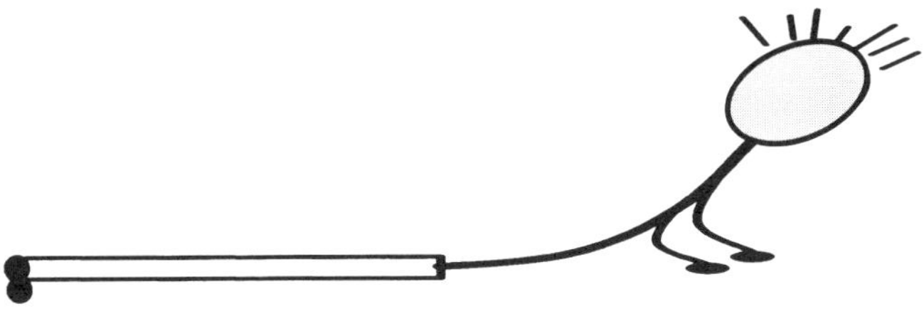

Figure 12 *Cobra Pose.*

1. Lie face down, with your forehead on the floor, legs and feet straight back (see Figure 13A).

2. Place your hands under your shoulder, fingers pointing inwards towards the other hand (see Figure 13B).

3. Use your back muscles to raise your head, shoulders, and chest off the floor in a smooth motion (see Figure 13C); do not use your arms to raise your body initially.

4. Next, use your arms to raise your body further off the floor. Keep elbows slightly bent, and your shoulders low (see Figure 13D).

5. Feel the stretch in your abdomen and the elongation in your spine. Hold the stretch for 10-15 seconds. Slowly increase duration to 30 seconds.

6. Return to the position, slowly lowering one vertebra at a time.

7. If there is pain or discomfort in performing this exercise, you may want to move your hands further in front of your shoulders.

Advanced Stage

After 4-6 weeks, perform the cobra pose with the following variation, with four additional steps.

1. Lie face down, with your forehead on the floor, legs and feet straight back.

2. Place your hands under your shoulder, fingers pointing inwards towards the other hand.

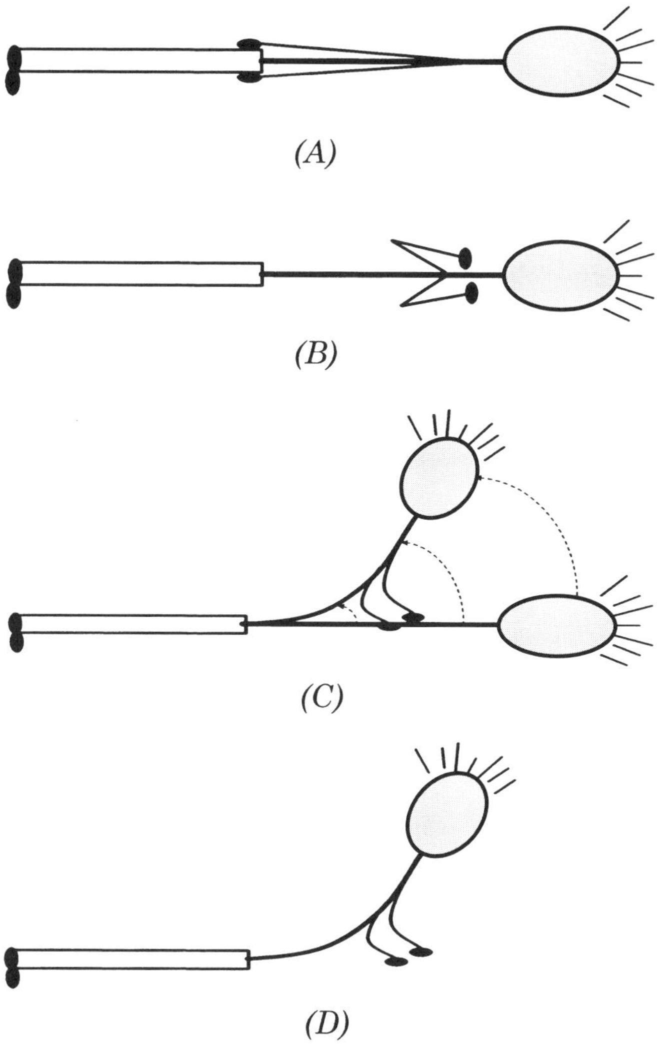

Figure 13 *Steps in Cobra Pose.*

3. Use your back muscles to raise your head, shoulders, and chest off the floor in a smooth motion; do not use your arms to raise your body initially.

4. Next, use your arms to raise your body further off the floor. Keep elbows slightly bent, and your shoulders low.

5. Feel the stretch in your abdomen and the elongation in your spine. Hold the stretch for 10-15 seconds.

6. Slowly bend your elbows, and lower your body slightly. Then look over your right shoulder towards your feet. Hold the stretch for 5 seconds.

7. Bring your face straight forward and use your arms to raise your body to the full extent again. Hold for 10 seconds.

8. Slowly bend your elbows and lower your body slightly. This time, look over your left shoulder at your feet behind you. Hold the stretch for 5 seconds.

9. Bring your face forward and use your arms to raise your body to the full extent. Feel that stretch in your abdomen. Hold the stretch for 10-15 seconds. Slowly increase duration to 30 seconds.

10. Return to the starting position, slowly lowering one vertebra at a time.

11. If there is pain or discomfort in performing this exercise, you may want to move your hands further in front of your shoulders.

Benefits

This pose removes tension from the spine and back, strengthens and firms the abdomen and buttocks.

Shoulder Stand

This pose, shown in Figure 14, requires strength and flexibility and should be undertaken after you have been practicing Yoga for a period of 5-6 weeks. It promotes circulation in the chest and neck. It also stimulates the glands, in particular the thyroid.

1. Lie flat on your back (see Figure 15A).

2. Place your hands at your sides, palms down, and begin to raise your legs (see Figure 15B).

3. Count to 10 as your legs are raised till they are vertical, and your legs are at a 90 degree angle to your back.

4. Press your hands against the floor to push your hips off the ground, pulling upwards with your legs.

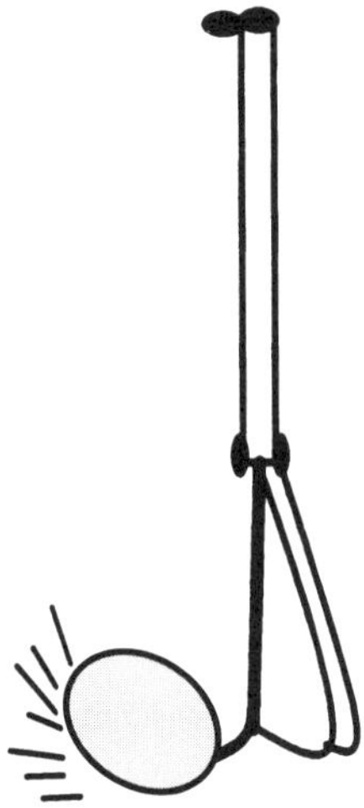

Figure 14 *Shoulder Stand.*

5. Place your hands on hips, elbows on the ground (see Figure 15C).

6. Keep your legs straight with toes pointing toward the sky.

7. Close your eyes and relax. Hold for 10 seconds.

8. Complete the exercise by first bringing your hips down to the floor.

9. Then lower your legs slowly to the ground.

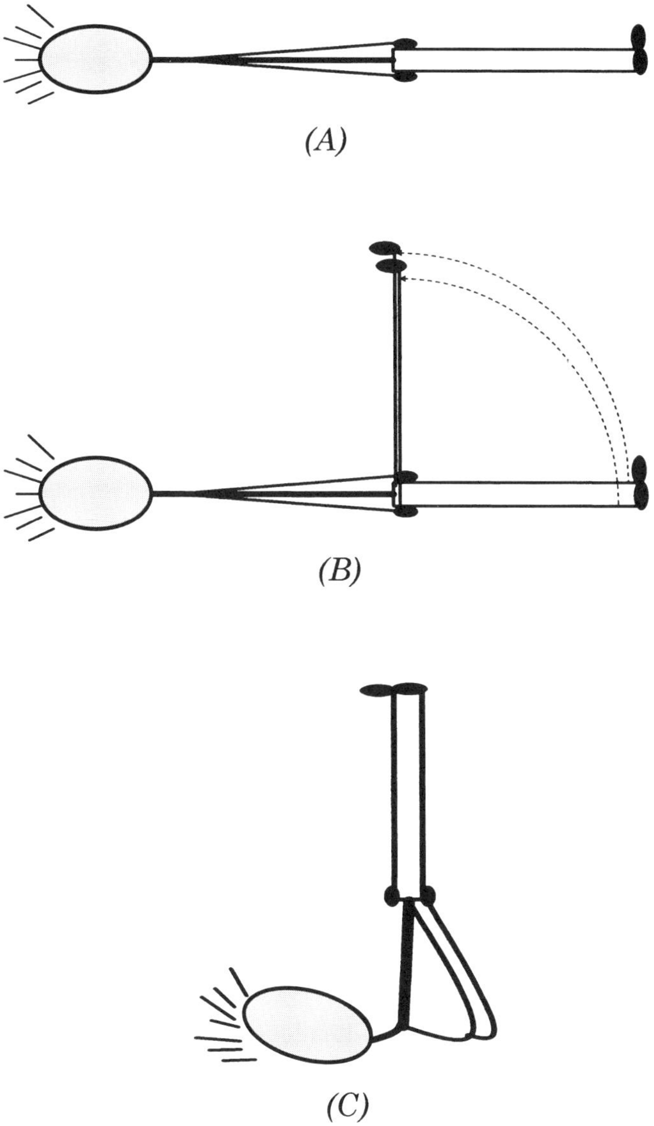

Figure 15 *Steps in Shoulder Stand.*

10. Lie still on your back in the relaxation pose for 1-2 minutes on completion of this exercise.

Benefits

The Shoulder Stand takes blood to the heart for purifying. Oxygenated blood circulates to the chest, relieving shortness of breath, asthma, throat ailments, anemia and fatigue. This pose stimulates the thyroid gland and soothes the nerves. It is, therefore, good for insomnia and relieving tension. It also aids digestion, helping heal ulcers and urinary disorders.

Plough

The Plough increases flexibility of the spine and is generally performed after the Shoulder Stand. It also provides extra blood to the internal organs. This pose is shown in Figure 16.

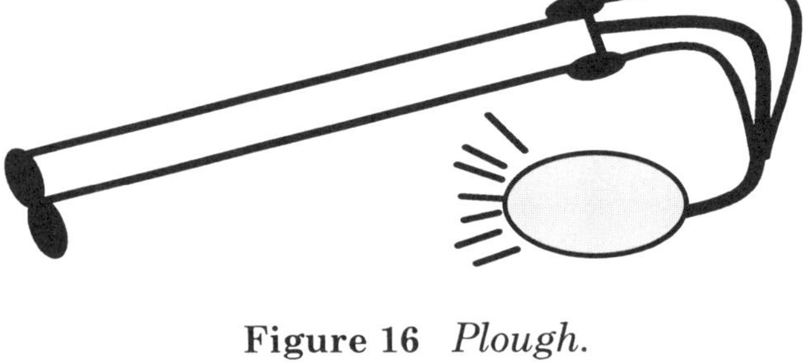

Figure 16 *Plough.*

1. Lie flat on your back with your arms by your sides.

2. Keep the palms of your hands on the floor (see Figure 17A).

3. Slowly raise your legs until they are vertical and at right angles to your back (see Figure 17B and Figure 17C).

4. Use your hands to push against the floor as you lift your lower back off the floor.

5. Continue lifting your trunk until your legs are lowered beyond your head (see Figure 17D).

6. Try to touch your feet to the ground behind your head. If there is discomfort, do not strain.

7. Your chin should be pressed against your chest (see Figure 17E).

8. Place your hands on your back with elbows on the ground. Hold for 15-30 seconds. Breathe normally.

9. Slowly uncoil your body, one vertebra at a time, until you return to the lying position on your back.

10. Take slow, deep breaths and relax for 1-2 minutes.

(A)

(B)

(C)

(D)

(E)

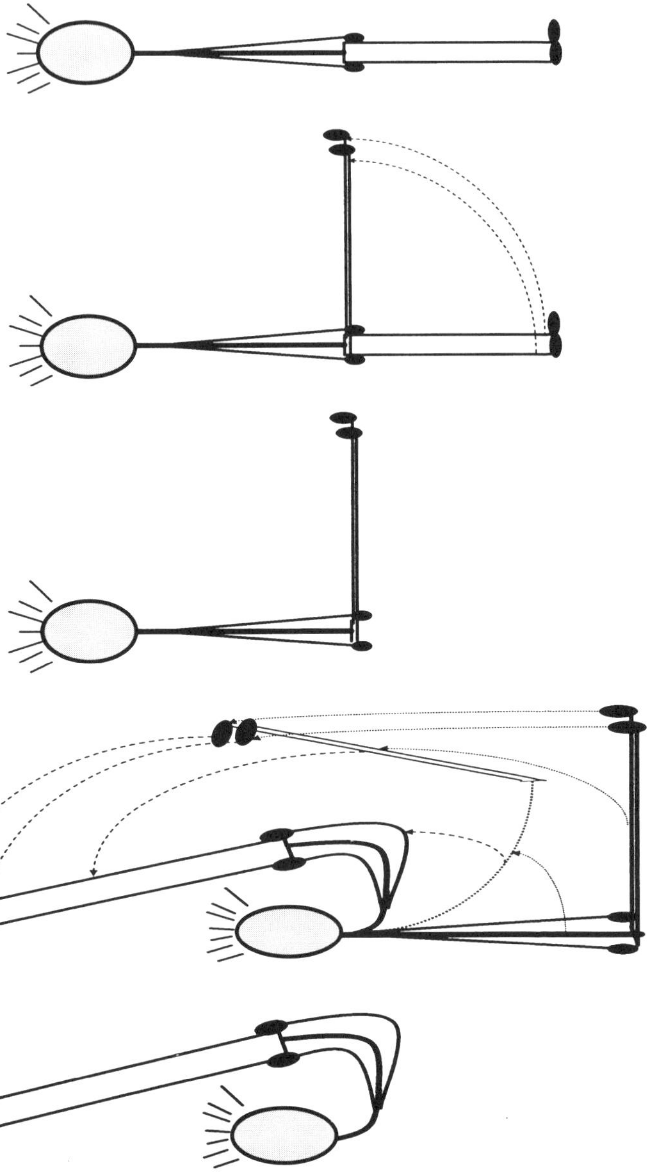

Figure 17 *Steps in Plough.*

Benefits

This increases flexibility of the spine and promotes deep relaxation of all the muscles. It also improves the functioning of the internal organs by supplying them with extra blood.

Bow

Each time you complete an exercise that bends your spine in one direction, it is recommended that you follow it with an exercise to bend it in the opposite direction. The Bow is generally performed after the Plough. The Bow pose is shown in Figure 18.

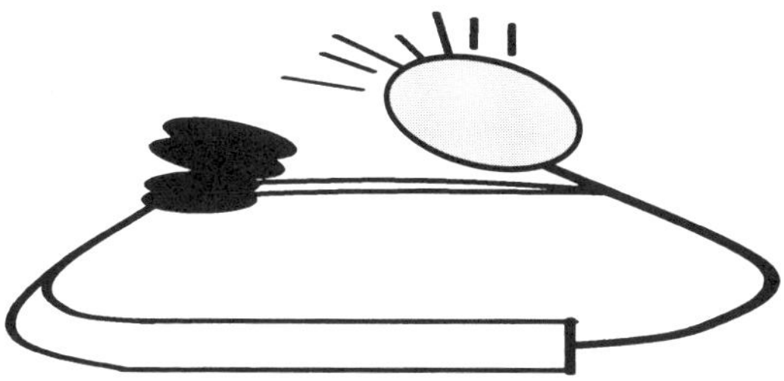

Figure 18 *Bow.*

1. Lie on your stomach with your arms by your sides.

2. Rest your chin on the floor (see Figure 19A).

3. Bend your knees keeping your feet together (see Figure 19B).

4. Reach your arms back and grasp your ankles (see Figure 19C).

5. Pull back with your feet, slowly raising your torso while arching your back (see Figure 19D).

6. Let your body weight fall on your abdomen.

7. Tilt your head back and hold the stretch for 10 seconds.

8. Slowly lower your torso, until chin is resting on the floor.

9. Let go off your ankles and lower feet to the floor.

10. Keep lying on your stomach with your head turned to one side, and rest.

Benefits

This exercise shapes and tones the hips, thighs, buttocks and abdomen. It strengthens the lower back and increases flexibility in the chest, shoulders, back and arms.

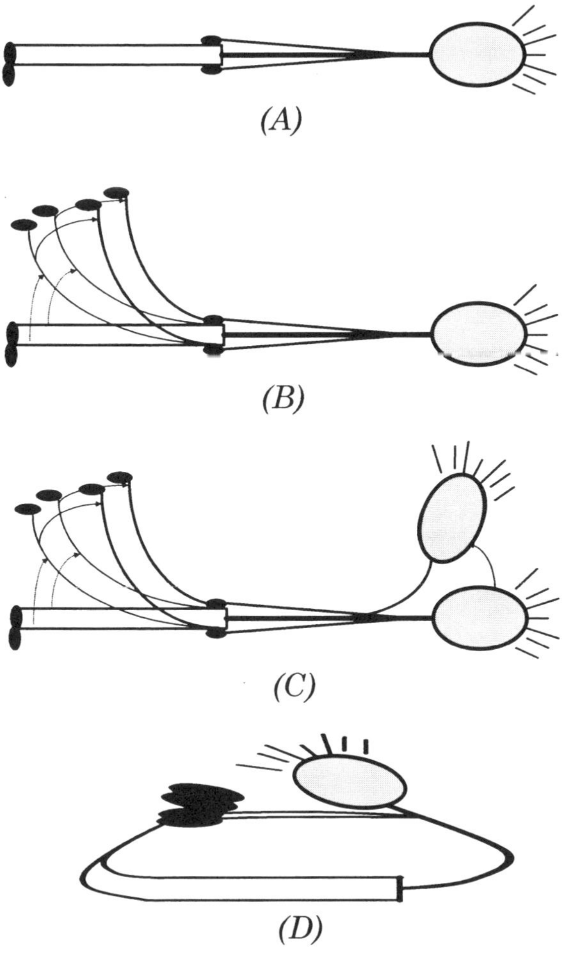

Figure 19 *Steps in Bow.*

Backward Bend

This exercise is used to increase flexibility in the ankles, feet and spine. The pose is shown in Figure 20.

Figure 20 *Backward Bend.*

1. Sit on the back of your heels with your feet close together (see Figure 21A).
2. Slowly move your arms backward, and place your hands on the heels.
3. Inhale and expand your rib cage, while arching your spine backward.
4. Hold position for 10 seconds.
5. Return to starting position, and relax for 10-15 seconds.

6. Next, move your arms backward, and place the hands on the floor behind you (see Figure 21B).

(A) (B)

Figure 21 *Steps in Backward Bend.*

7. Drop your head backward while inhaling and expanding your rib cage.

8. Arch your spine.

9. Hold stretch position for 10 seconds.

10. Walk hands forward, return to start, and relax.

Benefits

This increases flexibility in the ankles, feet, and spine. It also strengthens the abdomen and lower back.

Relaxation Pose

This is the most important exercise of all the ones mentioned in this text. Every attempt must be made to finish each Yoga session by spending at least 10 minutes in this pose. The pose is shown in Figure 22.

Figure 22 *Relaxation Pose.*

1. Lie flat on your back, with your heels shoulder distance apart, and feet falling outwards to the sides.

2. Your arms should be by your sides, palms facing upwards.

3. Relax your jaw, and close your eyes.

4. Your breathing should be soft and slow — no more than 4 breaths a minute.

5. Relax your entire being, starting with the feet and moving up to the face.

   a. Feel your heels and feet relax. Then your toes.

   b. Move upwards and feel your ankles, calves, and knees relax.

   c. Relax the quadriceps and hamstrings.

   d. Relax your back. Then the abdomen.

   e. Relax the chest muscles. Then the shoulders.

   f. Relax your arms, elbows, forearms, hands, and fingers.

   g. Relax the muscles in your neck.

   h. Relax your chin and mouth.

   i. Relax your face (cheeks) and the eyes.

As you go deeper into relaxation, feel that life-giving force go through your body to the very depths of your being. With each breath you take in, feel the energy flowing in you. With each exhalation, let the stress and tension flow out. Stay in that state of calm for about 10 minutes.

When rising from the relaxation pose, do so in a slow and deliberate manner. First move your toes and fingers; then rotate your wrists and ankles. With the next breath, stretch your arms and legs. After a few more breaths, roll to your side and sit up.

Benefits

This invigorates the body and mind through conscious relaxation.

Meditation Pose

This is the most relaxed and comfortable pose (other than the Relaxation Pose), and can be maintained for extended periods of time with only a little practice. It derives its name from the fact that it is most commonly used when meditating. The pose is shown in Figure 23.

1. Sit down in the cross-legged position, with spine straight.

2. Ensure that your knees are lower than your hips. This will enable you to keep your back straight without strain.

3. Perform deep breathing exercises.

   a. As you breathe in, maintain your focus on the breath as it passes through you. With each inhalation,

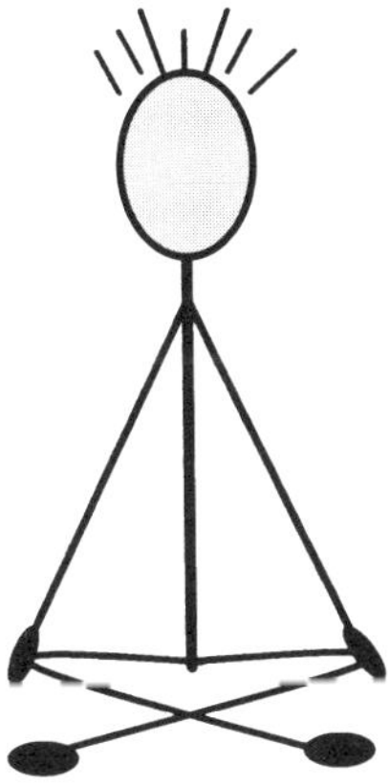

Figure 23 *Meditation Pose.*

feel that life-giving force go down to the very depth of your being.

b. As you exhale, feel all the toxins and stress leave your body.

c. Take no more than 3-4 breaths per minute.

d. Continue for a period of 15-20 minutes, keeping your mind on the long, slow breaths going in and out of your being.

The focus on the breathing is to keep the mind from wandering. As you become more disciplined, you no longer need to focus on your breathing. Instead, you start to feel that energy within you, and its connection to all things in nature. You start experiencing that power and the ability to channel it over time.

Benefits

The Meditation Pose helps relax the body and mind. It increases awareness of unity of mind and body.

Thought for the Day

STRETCH YOUR PHYSICAL AND MENTAL LIMITS!

Chapter 7

Exercise

Visit any bookstore or library and you will find a plethora of information on exercise. There are books and magazines galore talking about cardiovascular fitness, strength training and a host of related topics. This chapter is focused on how you can develop a program that works for you.

Exercise positively affects our physical, mental and emotional well-being. Consistent exercise transforms the body into strong, high-energy, lean muscle. Also, endorphins released during exercise help relax the mind and produce a state of emotional well-being. Exercise builds endurance, decreases body fat and helps release pent-up emotions.

Let us take a look at the four measures of physical fitness:

1. Endurance
2. Strength
3. Flexibility
4. Body Fat

To increase endurance, pick any aerobic exercise. It could be running, cycling, rowing, skiing, swimming or a class at the local gym. Whatever you do — Make it FUN! It is much easier to keep up something you enjoy doing. It is equally important to keep it simple. I enjoy running because of its inherent simplicity. All that's needed is a good pair of shoes and the ability to put one foot in front of the other. Yet jogging, with all its simplicity, may not be for you. Pick any exercise program that you can adhere to consistently.

Strength training is important at all ages. However, it becomes even more significant after the age of forty, as you lose muscle mass with each year thereafter. Lean muscle burns fat and provides one with high energy. Yet, many of us avoid strength training because it appears complex. One often gets intimidated by the gyms with their large machines and weight equipment. However, strength training can be done simply at home with a pair of dumbbells and a chin-up bar. Again, the rule is to keep it simple and fun!

For increased flexibility, get a good book on Yoga or pick from the exercises in the chapter on Yoga and develop your own pattern. You may decide to organize your flexibility exercises into two or three sets. Perform a different set of exercises each day. That way, you break the monotony of having to repeat the same exercises day after day.

As your endurance and lean muscle increases, your body fat will decrease. You can aid that process by supplementing your diet with a healthy dose of fruits, vegetables and nuts. More on this will be covered in the next chapter on healthful eating.

The first thing to keep in mind is that more isn't always better. I have known people plunge into a fitness program with great enthusiasm and drop it a few weeks later, after the initial charm has worn off. Very often, the reason is because they either are:

- unable to make the large time commitment on a long-term basis, or
- are dissatisfied with the results.

Let's deal with each of these factors in the light of this text. A practitioner of holistic health takes a balanced approach to improving his health, just as he does with all aspects of his life. He is not looking to buff up instantly to feed his ego or suddenly lose weight to appear slim. Instead, he looks at exercise as one factor to improve his lifestyle.

Through meditation, he is able to maintain his calm state of mind. With this approach, he is far more likely to ease into a program that can be sustained over the long haul. Just as a baby learns to walk before it can run, we need to recognize that any new undertaking requires a gradual transition. Easing into an exercise program serves multiple purposes:

- It gives you time to mentally adjust to the change.

- The musculoskeletal system gets time to adapt to the changes, thereby preventing injuries.

- The cardiovascular system becomes more efficient before you stress it unduly.

- Your expectations are better managed as you will not expect overnight results.

Before concluding this chapter, I would like to take away the excuse of the busy traveler. I know I travel and still manage to find time for a workout. One can adhere to an exercise regimen no matter which part of the world we are in. Most hotels around the worlds have gyms and swimming pools. There are other options:

- Climbing up and down the stairs provides a great cardiovascular workout.

- Stomach crunches and push-ups can be done in the privacy of your room.
- Last, but not least, there is always a road outside your hotel room to go for a walk or jog.

THOUGHT FOR THE DAY

EXERCISE YOUR OPTIONS FOR GREATER STRENGTH AND ENDURANCE!

Chapter 8

Healthful Eating — Power Foods

Consuming all the food in your refrigerator won't help, if you don't get the essential nutrients needed to maintain an active and healthy lifestyle! Eating from all the major food groups is obviously important. You need to get adequate quantities of vitamins (vegetables, fruits), protein (lean meats, grains, nuts), calcium (dairy products), and a host of other natural elements.

Equally important is the source of the five food groups. My son's views on nutrition a few years ago summed up the state of his diet. His idea of getting 2 serving of carbohydrates, protein, fruit, vegetable, and dairy:

- Burger/chicken sandwich: 2 servings of carbohydrates and protein.

- French fries with ketchup: 2 servings of vegetables.

- Large strawberry ice-cream: 2 servings of fruit and dairy.

While this appeared to satisfy the stipulated requirements of the food pyramid, his weight ballooned and he was low on energy. Fortunately, a rigorous running program at school, and his desire to earn the Personal Fitness merit badge as a scout, helped alter his food habits for the better.

When we cook food, we lose a lot of these valuable nutrients. For most of us, eating food that has not been fried, curried, or well-done, is not a natural thing. I had to work at incorporating raw fruits and vegetables in my diet. Even with the best of efforts, I struggled with getting in adequate servings of fruits and vegetables. That was generally true, until I started juicing. (Chapter 9 — Juicing)

It is widely accepted that a well-balanced diet is a key factor in maintaining good health. What is not apparent is that the proper digestion of food depends on the balance between the body, emotional state of the person, and the inner mind.

Let's take a look at what that means to you — a practitioner of holistic health as defined in this text.

- **Meditation** provides the basis for healthful eating. A person in touch with his/her inner mind has the right attitude towards food. It's the same balance he/she brings to everything in life. Being centered, there are few cravings. The individual eats the right kinds of food at the right time (for the most part).

- **Yoga** helps alleviate stress, providing emotional stability. The foods that people reach for during boredom, depression, anger, are generally not healthy (You are more likely to reach for chocolates or ice-cream, rather than fruits and vegetables at that time).

- A physically fit person, who **exercises** regularly, is more likely to go after foods that provide the nourishment he/she needs to follow that lifestyle. An active person will also eat the correct amount of food, since overeating would leave him/her feeling lethargic.

- You can actually eat your way to slimness by avoiding processed foods. The greater the processing, the lower the food value. When you start feeling low on energy, you consume more food. If it is highly processed, you don't get the energy boost you are looking for, and you eat more. It is a vicious cycle. Try a **diet** consisting of whole grains, raw fruits and vegetables — you will have limitless energy and be full of life.

THOUGHT FOR THE DAY

FEED THAT POWER WITHIN YOU!

Chapter 9

Healthful Eating — Juicing

I must admit that juicing was of no interest to me during my younger days. I believed I could get all the essential nutrients from eating regular meals. If I needed more energy, I ate larger portions or an extra meal. Through my teenage years and into my twenties and thirties, this approach seemed to work.

Around ten years ago, two major factors changed my thinking. First, I started traveling extensively, often eating while traveling to and from airports each week. I was also spending less time in meditation than in past years. Second, I was getting close to forty. The result was decreased energy and an increasing waistline.

I knew I was getting excessive helpings of fried foods, and was falling short on my servings of fruits and vegetables. It was easier to make up the deficit in fruit — I just added one helping of fruit at breakfast, lunch and dinner. Vegetables were another matter altogether. I just could not bring myself to eat raw vegetables, and steamed vegetables did not appeal to my palate either.

The choices appeared slim. I either had to miss out on essential nutrients, or try and swallow what was inherently unpleasant. Neither option was acceptable — the former was leading me in a downward spiral towards ill-health; the latter was not sustainable over the long haul. I needed an alternate solution.

Then, on a weekend visit to the local library with my kids, I came across a book on juicing. The boys were busy picking their favorite books and I had time on my hands. I started thumbing through the pages of this paperback, with dozens of recipes of fruit and vegetable juices. Some of them actually looked good! I checked out the book and headed home.

The next day, I went and bought a juicer. Then I set out for the supermarket and bought the desired fruits and vegetables. I had just taken away the reasons for any excuses. Cautiously, I picked a couple of recipes that read like they would appeal to my taste buds. What followed was one of the most defining moments in my life! I loved both the juices I tried on my first day. I had just discovered a way to get all the nutrients from raw foods.

The only question that remained was whether this would reverse my energy level. Only time would tell. In the meantime, I found the juices so delicious that I started juicing twice daily — morning and evening. In due course, I started experimenting with the recipes and savoring the freshness of these drinks.

In a matter of days, I found myself with the usual bounce in my step and lots of energy. I was able to sit straight in the morning and meditate for longer periods of time. This, in turn, helped center me and provide increased focus on well-being. I now had a new resolve — make "friends" with fruits and vegetables to enhance my overall health. The transformation had begun! I wondered how I had stayed away from these miracle drinks through most of my youth.

The juices I have tried are too numerous to list in this text. I will, however, mention a few of my favorites, along with the reasons for their selection. One obvious reason is that I have found each of them to be delicious. The stated benefits are not medically approved recommendations — only what I have read on the subject.

Ginger Delight

My all time favorite is the Ginger Delight. There are numerous variations of this remarkable drink that I have tried and each one is delightfully refreshing. The basic ingredients are as follows:

- 5 medium carrots
- 1 small apple
- ½ inch fresh ginger root

First juice the apple, then the ginger, followed by the carrots.

Benefit

I have used it to alleviate muscle pains and even cure shin splints. It builds the immune system and prevents colds. There are texts that stipulate that because it is rich in pectin and Vitamin C, it aids in carrying cholesterol out of the system. Ginger is a heat furnace and helps in burning fat.

A point to note here is that I generally do not mix fruits in my vegetable juices, with the exception of the apple.

- Add ½ beet to the Ginger Delight

Benefit

Beets are great for cleansing the liver. (NOTE: Beet juice by itself is too strong and the liver may be unable to handle it)

- Add a small handful of parsley

Benefit

Parsley has 3 times the Vitamin C of an orange. It also has calcium, iron, and magnesium.

Power Booster

Another favorite is the Power Booster. In place of the ginger, throw in a handful of spinach and a celery stalk to the carrots, apple, beet, and parsley.

- 5 medium carrots
- 1 small apple
- ½ beet
- 1 handful parsley
- 1 handful spinach
- 1 stalk celery

First juice the beet and apple, then juice the greens with the carrots.

Benefits

In addition to building the immune system, the addition of spinach provides anti-oxidants that slow the aging process, and may also reduce the risk of lung cancer.

Healthy Bones

The Healthy Bones drink is a great means of obtaining calcium directly from raw vegetables. The beneficial value of calcium is well documented in the formation and maintenance of strong, healthy bones.

First juice the apple; then the ginger; finally juice the greens with carrots.

- 5 carrots
- 1 apple
- 1-2 kale leaves
- 1 handful of parsley
- ½-1 inch ginger root

Benefits

Kale and parsley are rich in calcium, Vitamin K, magnesium, and boron. Vitamin K helps calcium absorption in the bones; magnesium helps strengthen the bones, and boron reduces calcium excretion.

- Add 3-4 spinach leaves to the Healthy Bones drink

Benefit

Provides you with the added iron, found in both spinach and parsley, making it a "Power Drink".

I usually start the morning with a Ginger Delight, or one of the other vegetable juices. It provides me with instant energy, and helps jump-start my day. On occasion, I have blended a fruit drink to start the day — the Morning Energizer.

Generally, I savor the fruit smoothies in the evening after a long day. This is strictly a personal preference, as I know many people who start the day with fruit drinks. Personally, I find it easier to use the blender and rig up smoothies at the end of a day.

I have used just about any fruit, and some of them make their way into a lot of juices: Mango, Banana, Orange, Peach, Strawberries, and Papaya. Here are a couple of easy-to-make favorites.

Morning Energizer

Throw in a couple of oranges, a banana, a few strawberries and a cup of organic apple juice into the blender for a delicious, refreshing drink.

- 2 medium oranges (peeled)
- 1 medium ripe banana
- 5-6 fresh strawberries (frozen strawberries work as well)
- 1 cup organic apple juice

Benefits

The white inner skin of the orange is rich in bioflavonoid. Combined with Vitamin C, it helps strengthen blood vessels. Builds immune system.

- Add 1 mango (or a cup of frozen mango pieces)

Benefit

Not only does it enhance the taste, it prevents dehydration.

Mango-Papaya Delight

A wonderful drink for alleviating heartburn, and general well-being.

- 1 mango
- 2 slices papaya
- 5 strawberries
- 1 banana

Benefits

Alleviates heartburn; increases blood circulation; improves complexion.

Juicing has done wonders for me. Give it a try. You might end up with increased energy, or just find some refreshing drinks that catch your fancy. Check out the books on juicing at the local library or visit your favorite book store. I believe it will be worth your time.

Here are a few titles to help you get started:

1. *Juicing For Life* by Cherie Calbom and Maureen Keane (1991: Avery Publishing).

2. *The Book of Raw Fruit & Vegetable Juices and Drinks*, William H. Lee (1982: Keats Publishing).

3. *Getting the Best out of Your Juicer*, William H. Lee (1998: McGraw-Hill).

4. *Raw Juice Therapy*, John B. Lust (1982: Benedict Lust Publications).

5. *The Joy of Juicing Recipe Guide*, Gary & Shelly Null (1992: Avery Publishing).

6. *The Juicing Bible* by Pat Crocker, Susan Eagles (2000: Robert Rose).

7. *The Complete Book of Juicing* by Michael T. Murray (1998: Prima Health).

8. *The Complete Juicer* by Lionel Martinez (1992: Running Press).

Enclosed in Appendix B are three tables that provide the following:

1. Table 1: Provides a list of juices with their ingredients, and the associated benefits.

2. Table 2: Lists which fruits and vegetables contain specific vitamins and trace elements, along with their benefits.

3. Tables 3, 4 & 5: Provides a list of nutrients in alphabetical order — and the foods that contain them.

Thought for the Day

NOURISH THE ENERGY WITHIN YOU!

Section IV

You Can Win

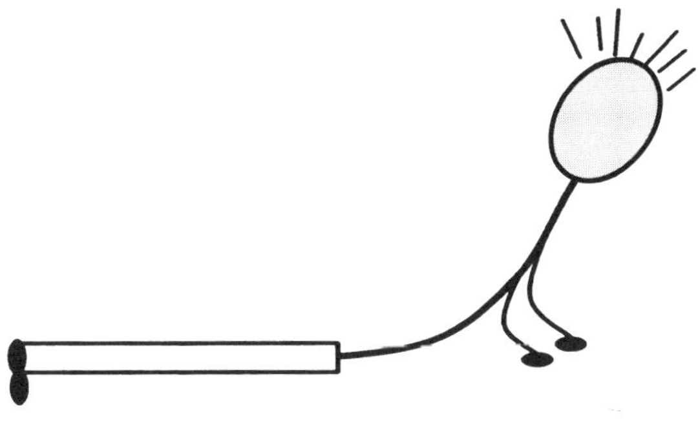

Chapter 10

Achieving Your Wellness Goals

How would you like to achieve your wellness goals without effort? Every time! What would you say if you knew you couldn't lose?

Let's take a look at reasons for failure of most plans. Most of us focus on one or more of the following:

1. *Diet* — Undue dependence on the diet results in self-deprivation, often leading to dissatisfaction. Reliance on any plan that leaves you ungratified is not sustainable. That is why most diets last only a

short time, followed by an urge to gouge, with predictable results.

2. *Exercise* — The focus is on the physical body, often ignoring the mind. Yet the two are inseparable. A majority of physical ailments are a result of stress and mental anguish. I may be in the best physical shape of my life, yet my morning run could be compromised under duress.

3. *Genes* — Attributing your state of health to genes means you can walk away from personal responsibility. It is easy to become a victim and claim it's outside your control. The reality is that no matter what your genes, you can take charge of your health and your life. You can't keep dining out and blame your parents for your weight.

4. *Excuses* — You can find a dozen excuses for something you choose not to do.

   a. "It's boring"

   b. "It's not my thing"

   c. "I don't have time"

   d. . . . Pick your favorite excuse

In each of the cases outlined above, the solution being sought is EXTERNAL to the individual. What's often ignored is the power of the mind. Through meditation and yoga, one can channel one's energy to a state of equipoise. You have to get past the I-N-T-E-L-L-E-C-T to the inner mind — the real YOU! Once that connection is established, you will feel a sense of satisfaction and well-being that will pervade every aspect of your life.

The mind is like a child, running in a thousand different directions. Through a combination of meditation and yoga, the mind can be relaxed. You can experience contentment and peace. The mind in this state is open to reception.

When you are in a relaxed state, you start taking control of your destiny. You begin to take responsibility for your actions. There is a balance that permeates every facet of your being. No longer is eating healthy an imposition, nor is it taken to extreme. You don't have to lose five pounds the first week. You know the results will follow in due course.

Being relaxed and centered allows you to put things in perspective and be content with what you have, so you can build on it. Contentment is a state of mind. No amount of physical or material goods can provide contentment. It has to come from within, through meditation. At that stage, the excuses disappear. You realize you are in control.

You can do anything you choose to do. You can, and will, succeed! For example, there is no need to jump-start an exercise program, and push through pain or injury. You can be patient and slowly build your endurance and strength. After all, you didn't get out of shape in a week. There is no reason to believe the reverse can be accomplished meaningfully. Stay within yourself, and you will achieve your wellness goals effortlessly.

THOUGHT FOR THE DAY

YOU CAN BE A WINNER EVERY TIME!

Chapter 11

The Choice is Yours

Think about this.

- Would you like to turn back the clock? Enjoy the endurance, strength, flexibility you enjoyed as a 25-year-old?

- Do you desire the weight and figure of your college days? No excessive body fat?

- Would you relish having the energy and bounce of a teenager? Not feel tired or exhausted all the time?

- Would you like to stay healthy on a regular basis? Alleviate back-pain and avoid recurring colds?

- Would you like to stay calm and relaxed? Not give in to excessive mood swings?

    ✧ Then you have to make some choices; some changes in your life.

The most important change is in your mind. YOU are responsible, and accountable, for your health and well-being. Are you ready to accept that?

It's a mindset shift. Once you make the decision to improve your health and your life, the rest is easy. It's easy provided your resolve to take responsibility for your well-being stemmed from the mind, the inner you! In order to do that, you have to first get in touch with yourself.

Take baby steps in the direction you want to proceed. The steps, and effort needed, are indeed small given the return on investment (ROI). Develop a plan.

For meditation or yoga

1. Set the time and place. Pick a time when you are feeling refreshed (for instance, after a good night's sleep).

2. Find a quiet place so there are no distractions.

3. Sit in a comfortable, relaxed manner (or perform the appropriate stretches).

4. Take long, slow, deep breaths.

5. Relax the mind (For greater detail, see the chapter on meditation).

For exercise

1. Decide on the time and place (Run in the park, sit-ups at home).

2. Determine the type of exercise you want to do (Endurance, Strength training).

3. Make it fun!

For healthy eating

1. List the foods you want to incorporate in your daily routine.

2. Start with a super breakfast — include fresh fruit & vegetable juices (they taste great, while providing you with the nourishment you need).

3. Get adequate protein in the form of lean meat, chicken, yogurt and nuts.

4. Get a good recipe book, so you don't get bored.

It's as simple as that. Just a few small steps and you could be on your way to a whole new different person. The key is meditation, which will enable you to relax and provide focus in your life. The choice is really YOURS!

THOUGHT FOR THE DAY

MAKE THE RIGHT CHOICE FOR YOU!

Chapter 12

Take Away the Excuses

Who amongst us has not found a reason to excuse ourselves when we opt to skip something that requires effort? Remind yourself that this is a commitment to your health, your well-being, your life. Each time you make an excuse, or are defensive about an action, there are negative ramifications. (YES! More than the one obvious one)

- The direct result is that you lose the benefit that would have accrued from following through (not excusing yourself).
- The real damage is that you become progressively weaker.

✧ In attempting to be smart, one outsmarts oneself. Being clever, you quickly learn to find ready excuses for not doing what's good for you.

✧ Without realizing, you become slave to the habit of rationalizing your actions.

It's the mind that becomes weak. With each excuse you make, you get weaker, and it becomes easier to lie to yourself the next time. Instead of making an effort, it becomes easier to give up — to walk away. One becomes a spineless weakling with ready-made alibis. How often have you heard the following:

- I can't wake up and meditate because I am a night person.
- I don't need IT.
- That's not me.
- I don't have time to exercise because of my job (yet one has time to watch TV).

How often have you heard that in today's day and age, there is no time to meditate, or exercise, or stop and smell the roses? There is a simple one-word response to such musings — TELEVISION!

Take away the television set and you will have time to get your life back together again. Initially, you might even wonder what to do with your newfound time. You might experience emptiness, a void, in your life. Take heart! Just as air rushes into a vacuum, you will find numerous things to do in that time. What you have done is eliminated your biggest excuse — lack of time!

Proceed with caution! You don't want to replace the TV with the phone or something similar — leaving you without time to do the activities important for your well-being, and your life. The good news is that you have a clean slate to start from. Now is the time to channel your energies into meaningful pursuits.

All you have to do is take the time to sit down, close your eyes, breathe deeply, and reflect on who you want to be. Do it slowly and in a relaxed manner. Feel the life giving force flow through you with each breath you take. In the calmness that follows, make your resolve to strip away the excuses and reach your full potential. You owe it to yourself!

You now have the time to be the best you can be — physically, mentally, spiritually. Are you ready to accept the challenge? Only you can decide. It is up to you.

THOUGHT FOR THE DAY

YOU CAN MAKE TIME FOR ANYTHING YOU WANT!

Section V

Applications to Daily Life

Chapter 13

Managing Risk — Weight and Diabetes

We hear so much about our genetic disposition, that we start believing we are doomed to failure should we try to defy the odds. This is ingrained into us from early childhood by well-meaning family, friends and the plethora of medical information surrounding us.

I write from experience because I grew up with the knowledge that diabetes and heart disease were a part and parcel of our lives. My paternal side of the family has had type 2 diabetes for generations and my maternal side of the family has heart disease. My father has lived with severe diabetes for over 30 years, with severe complications including eye hemorrhage and loss of vision. My mother has been an angina patient for more than 20 years.

I have always had a tendency to put on weight, which I conveniently attributed to my genes. It was easy to ignore that I overate at parties, often putting away half a dozen desserts after having eaten enough for a week. I chose to be irresponsible and the world had provided me with a crutch — it wasn't my fault but that of my genes. It was like the genes had taken on a life of their own and I had no control over my health and my life.

Being an engineer by training and profession, I believed in the physical sciences. I had come to believe that I had a predisposition towards certain ailments. What was worse was the rationalization that while I could make some changes in my lifestyle, I could never really be carefree and healthy.

The very thought of being a slave to my genes was upsetting. This, in turn, affected my response to the situations around me. If I was going to have heart disease, why not indulge myself till I dropped. Of course, the more I gave in to my cravings, the worse the situation became. I was making it a self-fulfilling prophecy!

The saving grace for me was that I had been introduced to meditation at a very young age. As I sat in contemplation during the wee hours one morning, totally at peace with myself and all of creation, I had a feeling of well-being. I was no longer weighted down with the fear of these genes running through my body, causing havoc at every turn in my life. I knew right then and there that I could be well.

I couldn't control my genes, but I could control my response and the resultant benefits that accrued to me. First and foremost, the realization that I could influence my well-being helped me relax. With that came the ability to think clearly and plan a course of action unemotionally. It wasn't easy — my eating habits weren't the best. Fried foods and desserts are still favorites of mine. I did not eliminate anything from my diet. What I did was two-fold:

- Instead of 4-6 desserts at a party, I would eat a couple of them. That way, I did not feel deprived.

- I started the day with a healthy breakfast. This provided me a good start and usually kept me from the munchies till later in the day.

What is of greater significance is that being relaxed had a far greater impact than the change in my eating habits. Since I believed deep down that I was going to be healthy, my physical body started responding to it. My body functions started mirroring what was inside me. I am convinced that more than seventy-five percent of the benefits resulted from my state of mind. After all, I had attempted to control my eating earlier, with far poorer results.

The weight started dropping off. This gave me newfound hope and increased my resolve to better myself. Through meditation, I was centered. What I did was not out of desperation or a state of panic, but in a calm, relaxed manner. Now, I decided to minimize the chances of falling prey to diabetes, given the family history. Numerous articles on the subject had shown that a regular exercise program could keep diabetes under control. I started on a modest jogging program of 6 miles a week. Over time, I built on it.

My focus continues to be one of calming the inner mind. All our energies emanate from it. The physical body responds to it. When at peace, the inner mind will bring the physical, mental, and emotional energies to a state of equilibrium.

My cholesterol is by no means optimal. I know further improvement is needed, but I am secure in the knowledge that I am in a better position than I used to be, without the use of medication. I have no signs of diabetes, my weight is regulated, and I have limitless energy. I also know that in the rare event of my falling sick, I recover rapidly because of my state of mind.

You too can transform your life. You don't have to be controlled by your genes. You can improve every aspect of your life. Take it from someone who had to work on weight problems, cholesterol, and the heavy hand that was genetically dealt.

THOUGHT FOR THE DAY

YOU HAVE THE POWER TO HEAL YOURSELF!

Chapter 14

Turning Back the Clock

Remember the time when you had boundless energy? When you were physically fit and could accomplish what you can only dream of now? Ever thought about what it would be like to experience that feeling again? What would you give to partake of that elixir of youth — the magic potion — that would transform you into that specimen of years gone by?

You have it in you to reverse the aging process. The first step is to recognize that you have the potential to be the person you choose to be. Then plan on a course of action, one small step at a time. It's that simple, really!

Let's see what we were like as kids. I know I could run around for hours playing games (endurance). I could stick my toe in my mouth (flexibility). As a teenager, I was called upon to help move heavy objects (strength). And I probably had far less body fat 25 years ago.

The four measures of physical fitness are:

- Endurance
- Flexibility
- Strength
- Body Fat

There are very few people that are truly fit. Even Olympians don't always fit the bill because they focus on one element to the detriment of others. There are weight lifters who can't run around the block. There are marathoners who can't touch their toes. It is important to recognize this distinction.

As children, we ran, we played. We had FUN! Each day, I tried to do better than I had done the previous day. I exulted when I could hit the ball a little further, or run a lap around the track a little faster than the last time. I measured myself against what I had accomplished recently. Even though I raced or played against others, the only person I really competed with was myself.

Along the way to adulthood, I lost track of that very important perspective. I started competing against others. What that did was affect my mind. Instead of continuing to grow to the best of MY abilities, I was obsessed with how I could win against others. In a sense, I kept trying to live up to someone else's potential. Therein lay the problem.

Through meditation, I was able to get in touch with the child within me, the being that had not yet been influenced by the outside world. As I centered and relaxed, I recognized that each of us is special in our own way. I could grow to my full potential. I may not be a world-class runner or swimmer, but I owed it to myself to be in the best shape of my life, to be healthier than I had ever been.

I was then able to embark on a plan that touched on the cornerstones of a healthy lifestyle, with meditation providing the pivot.

- Through **meditation**, I continued to stay calm, relaxed and focused. This prevented me from setting unreasonable goals or striving for instant results. I was going to turn back the clock and I had my life to do it.

- For flexibility, I did **yoga** and stretching each day. The breathing exercises help in relaxation and the stretches ensure my musclcs continue to be supple, thereby minimizing the risk of injuries.

Figure 24 *Meditation is the Pivot.*

✧ To build endurance, I started on a running program that grew over time from a modest total of 6 miles per week to 15, and to 30+. I have completed a few marathons, though I do them not to compete, but for the sheer joy I get from the feeling of being young again.

Push-ups, sit-ups and light weights form the basis of my strength training program, complementing my running for a complete **exercise** regimen.

- Body fat has decreased as a result of all of the above and a few minor changes to my eating habits. I drink fresh vegetable or fruit juices to supplement my **diet**. This gives me the added energy I need to exercise.

Today, I have greater endurance, more flexibility, and lower body fat, than I had 25 years ago during my college days. My upper-body strength is not where it is used to be, but I am confident I will get there. I may never win a race, but I am secure in the knowledge that I am living up to my potential.

By going within yourself and drawing on your energy source, you can utilize the power of your inner mind to turn back the clock and savor the joy of youthfulness once more.

Thought for the Day

THE ELIXIR OF YOUTH IS IN YOUR MIND!

Chapter 15

Marathoning

Running continuously for 26.2 miles seems like a long way! I generally don't drive that far in a day. Yet thousands of people run marathons each year. What gets them to the finish line? More importantly, what gets them to the starting line? The desire to look better, feel better? That can be achieved with far less effort, through cross-training. Most runners I have talked to have said it is the intrigue of the marathon. It's the point past the 18-21 mile mark, where you have to dig deep into yourself.

I can say the same for myself. The marathon is where I have come to draw on my inner strength in its rawest form — physical energy. Studies havc shown that around the 20-mile mark, your glycogen resources are depleted. All you have left is what is inside you. For a student of meditation and power of the inner mind, that is beautiful! It is yet one more illustration of the bountiful energy within you just waiting to be tapped.

Figure 25 *Marathoning.*

I am by no means a speedster. I run the event at a 9-10 minute per mile pace. Due to other commitments in life — I am a Scoutmaster for our local troop, work at a high-tech Silicon Valley Company, and have a family with 3 children — I have to be flexible with my marathon training. I try to get in a long run of 20+ miles before the marathon, although I have gone in with less than that a couple of times.

What I do have going for me is the ability to relax. I can go deep into myself and actually visualize crossing the finish line. It is this feeling I draw on in all aspects of my life, and the marathon certainly gets me to utilize it to the fullest.

You may or may not ever run a marathon. It is important to realize that you have the power within you to unleash this extra energy for any marathon task in your daily life. You can utilize it for chores after an unusually long day at work. Or you may draw on it to take care of a sick child without losing your cool.

I don't want to upset marathoners all over the world by implying equivalency. I am not trivializing the marathon. What I am suggesting to readers is that each of us has choices to make in defining our marathon goals. Maybe some of you will decide to run a marathon in the future. Good for you! You can rest assured that you will be able to utilize the power you have harnessed to meet your running goals as well. Happy trails!

THOUGHT FOR THE DAY

YOU CHOOSE YOUR MARATHON GOALS IN LIFE!

Chapter 16

Managing Stress

We all experience ups and downs in our daily lives. In most cases, how we respond to each situation determines whether the experience will be stressful or not. There will always be exceptions to the rule as in when you are framed, or someone is slanderous towards you — it is normal to experience anxiety in such cases. Even then, it is possible to minimize the stress and the effect it has on you and your well-being.

Think about this. When I give in to feelings of negativity towards someone, I am affecting my health, because I have chosen to let my consciousness stray from its state of equipoise. What is even more ironic is that I have given control of my health and well-being to someone else — someone I may not respect!

The person who cares most about your health is — YOU. You owe it to yourself to learn to relax at every opportunity you get. You can practice at home, on the freeway, at work. Here are some techniques I have used to advantage.

- On waking:
  - ✦ Slowly stretch and savor the joy of being alive.
  - ✦ Wash, and meditate — to experience the calm and quiet in your mind.
  - ✦ Exercise — Go for a jog or do yoga to alleviate any physical tension.
- When driving:
  - ✦ Pause when agitated on the road. Take a deep breath and relax.
  - ✦ Be glad you have a car to move around in.
- At work:
  - ✦ Check periodically to see if the mind steers clear of negative thoughts.
  - ✦ Take a break and stretch; re-fill your water bottle.
  - ✦ Think about the fun things on the job.

- With children:
    - ✦ Instead of "being driven up a wall", think of the joy they bring.
    - ✦ Learn to listen, and they will listen in turn.
- At night:
    - ✦ Before retiring, dwell on the magic of the day.
    - ✦ Think of all the things that went right.
    - ✦ Be grateful for yet another opportunity to savor life.

Meditation is the key to calming the inner mind. This is the most important aspect of leading a relaxed and virtually stress-free life. I say "virtually" because even the most centered mind can get perturbed. However, the greater the time spent in meditation, the quicker the mind recovers when dislodged from its state of equilibrium. It will help provide focus and enable you to maintain your calm, and healthful, lifestyle. Keep in mind that stress contributes to:

- ✦ Back pain
- ✦ High blood pressure
- ✦ Heart attacks

- . . . (Numerous other maladies)

You can choose what you want. Happiness is a state of mind, and your emotional state will determine your physical well-being.

Here are some pearls I turn to repeatedly for stress management:

- **Never hurry!** (to the point where it causes anxiety)
- **Never worry!** (over events outside your immediate control)
- **There is nothing important in life!** (to fret over, and cause distress)
- **Have no regrets!**

Very simple, yet effective at managing stress!

THOUGHT FOR THE DAY

RELAX YOUR WAY TO A HEALTHIER YOU!

Chapter 17

Project Management

Project Management is less about plans, schedules, and indicators, than most people would have you believe. Yes, I have utilized these traditional widgets, but that is not the reason for the success of my best projects. The primary reason for the success of any program — be it a worldwide development project with hundreds of people, or a local community project — is the emotional rapport I have struck with other members of the project team.

In my experience, there are actually very few issues. Team members tend to agree on 95% of the features. Yet the focus rapidly shifts to the 5% of the items people disagree on, leading to confrontation, polarization, and distrust. This is a direct result of individuals viewing the disagreements as personal attacks on themselves. When you take things personally, there is the feeling of a lack of respect for your ideas, resulting in anger and shutting out the other point of view.

You project what's inside you. When there is turbulence within, it will be displayed as a reactionary force. When the inner mind is calm and collected, you will radiate positive energy. This energy forges a connection with those around you. It negates any animosity and antagonism and replaces it with a feeling of trust and friendship. Now you are working jointly to resolve the issues — it is no longer "me" versus "you".

Start projecting this force in a one-to-one situation initially. Unless you are truly centered and really tapped into your inner mind, it is easier to establish a connection with one energy source as opposed to many. There are people that can establish this connection with every person in the room. You have to be in a state of calm and equipoise that comes with years of meditation and practice.

No matter which mode you use to get connected, the results are the same. You increase your chances of achieving resolution and meeting your program targets. The question then becomes — What can you do to harness that energy and project it for success?

Even though I mention meditation as a primary means of relaxation, the whole cycle of meditation, yoga, healthful eating, and exercise, reinforce and support one another. This is shown in Figure 26.

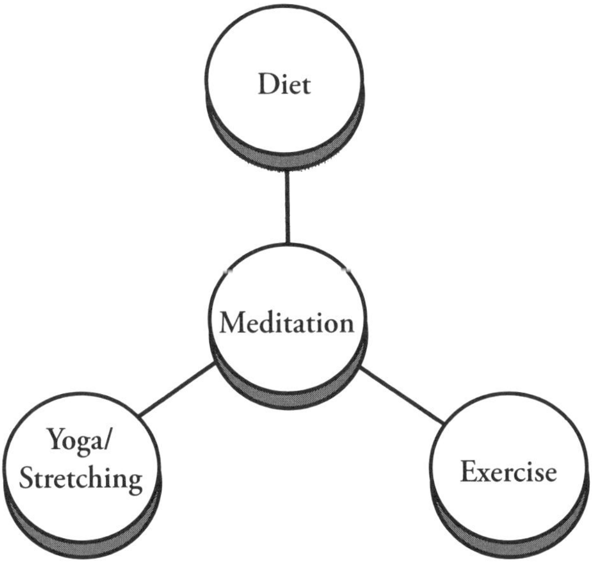

Figure 26 *Pillars of Holistic Health.*

- Meditation helps you relax, so you can retain focus on the other pillars of holistic health (yoga, diet, exercise) and your program goals (stress management, marathoning, etc.).

- Yoga helps the different parts of the body and the internal organs to become physically whole (Aiding in digestion and performance of endurance exercise).

- Healthful eating provides the right nutrients and nourishment (So the individual can exercise and function efficiently).

- Exercise helps release pent-up emotions (So you can sit quietly in meditation).

Each of these cornerstones builds on and supports the others. It is meditation that holds it all together, providing the focus to follow other programs. By doing this consistently, you will get in touch with your inner mind and be able to channel your energy for succeeding in all aspects of your life — project management being just one of the programs.

THOUGHT FOR THE DAY

CHANNEL YOUR POSITIVE ENERGY FOR SUCCESS!

Section VI

Synthesizing Holistic Health

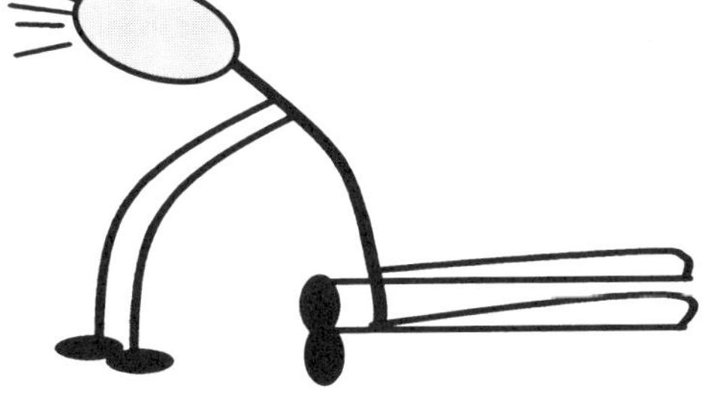

Chapter 18

Step-By-Step Guide

Most of us would not run our businesses with a low Return on Investment (ROI). Yet we continue to operate physically, mentally, and emotionally, at five to ten percent of our abilities. It is indeed ironic that our most valuable asset — our well-being — is wasted away daily.

In order to function more effectively, what's needed is to bring the entire being to operate in unison. Recognition of the oneness of mind and body forms the basis for growth. In the remainder of this chapter, you will go through a number of exercises to aid you in your journey towards complete health.

The success of this program depends on your current state of mind. The more relaxed you are, the easier it will be to delve deeper into your consciousness, and the more rapid will be your progress. In order to relax, you need to meditate. It seems like a vicious cycle — You need to relax to be able to meditate, and meditate to relax your mind. How do you break the cycle? Let's take a look at how we can increase the odds in our favor.

The first step is to pick a suitable time when you:

- Have at least 30 minutes,
- Are well rested, and
- Expect minimal distraction/disturbance.

The morning generally works well in this regard for most people, although any time that fits your lifestyle and meets the conditions is suitable.

To increase the chances of being rested in the morning, I recommend starting the process the previous evening. Before retiring for the night, try and do the following:

- Minimize food intake the last 60-90 minutes prior to bedtime.
- Massage your forehead, temples, lower back, and soles of feet.

✦ Use the appropriate oil for your body type (Appendix A):

- Vata — Calming Oils
- Pitta — Cooling Oils
- Kapha — Burning Oils

✦ After lights out, sit up straight in bed and take 7-10 deep breaths.

✦ Dwell for a few moments on the pleasant things that happened during the day.

✦ Gently lie down and sleep.

On waking in the morning:

✦ Slowly stretch your legs/feet straight out in one direction, and arms over your head in the opposite direction. Take a deep breath while you stretch. Breathe out and relax. Repeat 3 times.

✦ Wash your face, hands, and feet with cool water.

✦ Lightly massage your temples and feet.

✦ Perform the mountain yoga exercise (Rising on your toes with arms and hands stretched skywards) 5 times.

- Sit down in the cross legged position, with spine straight, and perform deep breathing exercises. With each intake of breath, feel that life-giving force go down to the very depth of your being. Take no more than 3-4 breaths per minute. Continue for a period of 15-20 minutes, keeping your mind on the long, slow breaths going in and out of your being.

- Lie down on your back with your arms by your side and continue deep breathing for a few more minutes.

- You are now ready to start the rest of your day.

There is no better way to jump-start the rest of your day than with a power breakfast. A nourishing breakfast fuels you for the better part of the day, minimizing the desire to reach for unhealthy snacks. In addition to complex carbohydrates, it is important to get live foods into your system through vegetable and fruit juices. A sampler could include the following:

- Start with the Ginger Delight juice.

    - Carrots, apple, ginger

- Follow with a bowl of whole-grain cereal.

- Yogurt with fresh fruit can round off the meal.

There is a direct correlation between our energy levels and state of mind. When you are low on energy, it is difficult to maintain equilibrium and a calm state of mind.

Through the day, practice relaxing at every opportunity you get. It needs to be done consciously at first. Over time, it becomes as natural as breathing. Here are a few things to get you started:

- When driving, be aware you don't let traffic congestion or other drivers upset you.
- At work, check to see if the mind is dwelling on the negative; Return your focus to the fun aspect of the job.
- With children, instead of reacting to their antics, become carefree like them.
- At night, dwell on the joys of the day; Be thankful for another opportunity to experience life.

Relaxation is probably the most important aspect of this program. Through meditation, and yoga, you will attain equipoise. This will provide focus and enable you to maintain your exercise, healthful eating, and well-being lifestyle.

A word on physical exercise is in order at this point. Make it FUN! It is much easier to keep up something you enjoy doing. It is equally important to keep it simple.

About 15 years back, I fell into the trap of establishing an exercise routine that was doomed to failure from the onset. I enjoyed racquet sports and had set up times with different people to play squash, tennis, and badminton, through each week. With the best of intentions, I started missing workouts, due to one of the following:

- Partner had to cancel due to personal commitments.
- I was unable to make it at the appointed time, due to work schedules.
- Unavailability of courts at the time.
- Family needs in the evening (which is when my partners were available).
- Business travel to locations with lack of facilities/training partners.

I knew something needed to be done to increase my chances of exercising consistently. I looked at the factors that prevented me from completing my workouts and came to one simple conclusion. If I could find a way to exercise in the morning (while the family was sleeping), and could do it alone (when partners were unable to show up), I would have taken away my excuses.

I did not want to get to a gym in the morning with its blaring music and excessive noise. After meditation, I wanted to savor the peace and quiet for a while. It didn't take long to figure out the answer — jogging! It was as simple as putting one foot in front of the other. I did not need a partner every time I ran, although it was preferred. It could be accomplished in the morning, before the demands of daily life took over. There was always a road outside my hotel room wherever I traveled.

Running to me, has become moving meditation. After about 15 minutes, I am totally relaxed and breathing deep. Given that I generally run at a nature trail, the mind is free to take in the sights and sounds of nature. The hardest part is starting out. I always feel great when I am done.

Jogging, with all its simplicity, may not be for you. Pick any exercise program that you can adhere to consistently. Remind yourself what it does for you:

- Strengthens heart (Provided its aerobic in nature).
- Improves posture.
- Relieves stress.

- Reduces weight, etc.

With each of these benefits, you will be able to sit for longer periods in meditation. This, in turn, will help you get in touch with your inner mind. You will be able to draw on that power within you to transform your life and accomplish tasks which were beyond your reach just a few weeks earlier. The pillars of meditation, yoga, healthful eating, and exercise will reinforce each other, as you grow towards your full potential.

THOUGHT FOR THE DAY

CHANNEL YOUR ENERGY TODAY — AND GROW!

Chapter 19

Personal Glimpses

As I complete the final chapter of this book, I would like to share with you some wonderful, personal experiences. This is an attempt to illustrate what each of you can attain through the power of your mind.

Fastest Marathons

I ran my three fastest marathons in the past year to celebrate my upcoming fiftieth birthday. In the past, I always took a few days/weeks off from running to recover from the rigors of training for, and running, a marathon. After my last marathon, I experienced very little soreness and did five workouts the week following the run. I avoided the elevator and climbed up and down 6 flights of stairs the day after the marathon at work. (For those of you familiar with marathon lore, it is extremely painful to climb down stairs for a few days after the marathon).

I have run a marathon after having spent the preceding week in bed with the flu. Three weeks later, I was back at the starting line of another marathon with a knee that was still sore from the strain of running a marathon while recuperating from the cold. Well-meaning friends felt I was going to hurt myself. They believed I was risking permanent injury.

I was merely putting into practice what I had learned over the years.

- It is possible to control how much pain you feel — and your reaction to it!
- You can sensitize your being to determine the difference between discomforting pain, and the pain that could result in an injury!
- When you are in a state of calm equipoise, you can channel your inner mind to push the envelope of your abilities, yet restrain yourself to prevent injury!
- With each experience, you feel the energy within you grow by leaps and bounds!

Of course, the first run might have been more pleasant had I not been smitten with the flu, and gone into it with dead legs. The second one would certainly have been easier if I had allowed myself time to recover. However, I would have not had the opportunity to tap into this energy source and experience that power within me. I have found an endless source of energy that I am able to use in every facet of my life.

Back Pain

I know of many people around me who are afflicted with severe back pain. I believe most of them would benefit greatly from following a path of holistic health as outlined in this text. Through the practice of meditation and yoga/stretching, I have beaten the odds successfully.

Eighteen years earlier, I severely sprained my back while playing tennis. I was in excruciating pain for several days and had to be helped from my bed for the simplest of tasks. I was told that poor posture — crouching over a computer — had contributed to a weak back, and that I would have to be cautious the rest of my life. Deep down in my consciousness, I knew that could not be right. Against the advice of family and friends, I started stretching and strengthening exercises within a week.

I started waking up earlier each morning. In the pre-dawn hour, I meditated for a period of 30-60 minutes. This was followed by stretching/yoga. Within weeks, I could run and play racket sports without a hint of the back pain. I felt great!

Less than 2 years later, my car was rear-ended at a traffic light, causing severe whiplash to my back and neck. I had heard stories of recurring pain after such an accident. The pain also brought back memories of my previous injury. However, I had no hesitation this time on the path I was going to follow. Through meditation, yoga, and exercise, I was on my road to recovery in no time.

Today, my back is better than it's ever been. I have greater flexibility and strength than I have had during the preceding 20 years. It's comforting to know that I can go out and do whatever I want without giving a thought to whether my back could handle the strain.

Less Sick

I fall sick less frequently — my bout with the flu was the first one in many years. When I do experience an illness, it is short-lived. I have come to realize that as long as I am relaxed and in high spirits, there is very little that can affect me. In a sense, we cause a lot of the maladies that afflict us. When the inner mind is calm, it projects that energy through the rest of our being. Through meditation, you can achieve a sense of equipoise and quiet strength, which will open up doors for you in every aspect of your life.

THOUGHT FOR THE DAY

YOU CAN ACHIEVE OPTIMAL HEALTH — PHYSICAL, MENTAL, SPIRITUAL!

Appendix

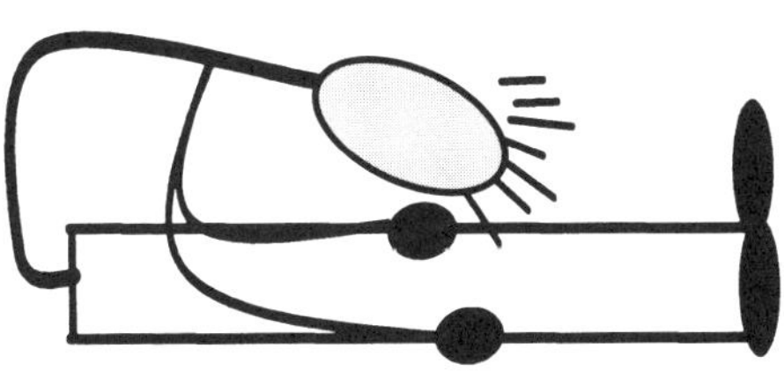

Appendix A

Ayurveda and Health

No compilation on holistic health would be complete without touching on some aspects of Ayurvedic science. Of course, a comprehensive exposition on Ayurveda is outside the scope of this text. There are volumes written, and four-year degree programs offered, on the subject.

In this chapter, I will attempt to present a brief summary of the physical, mental, and emotional disposition of the three body types. According to Ayurvedic science, all human-beings fall into one of three categories:

1. Vata

- Thin body, little weight gain.
- Teeth prone to decay.
- Eats irregularly.
- Suffers from insomnia.
- Given to restlessness.
- Nature's worrier: anxiety, tension, depression.

Raman's Holistic Health Response

- If you have this body type, you need to meditate on a daily basis. Meditation is the key to calming the inner mind. This will help you get centered and prevent depression. Throughout the day, make a conscious effort to steer your mind clear of negative thoughts.
- Before sleeping, you may want to drink a carrot-celery-parsley juice. All three are good sources of calcium and magnesium, the lack of which causes wakefulness.
    - 3-5 carrots
    - 3 celery stalks

- 1 handful parsley

Juice the celery first; then the parsley with the carrots.

❍ You need to practice deep breathing exercises to alleviate anxiety and tension.

2. Pitta

✦ Medium body.

✦ Thin hair, easily falls out.

✦ Good appetite, though not prone to rapid weight gain.

✦ Excessive perspiration.

✦ High intelligence — tendency towards anger and being judgmental.

✦ Displays leadership qualities; decisive.

Raman's Holistic Health Response

❍ If you have this body type, you need to meditate to dispel anger. Even if it is for a few minutes each morning (or evening), sit down quietly and reflect on the joys of life. As you give thanks, bring your mind to the energy within you. Relax and feel it flow through your being. Experience the calm and tranquility. Take away the anger and judgment.

- With excessive perspiration, you need to make a conscious effort to prevent dehydration. Drink the Morning Energizer with mango (see chapter on Juicing). Also, consume at least eight glasses of water each day.

3. Kapha

- Body prone to fat.
- Tendency to oversleep.
- Resistant to change.
- Clinging and greedy in personal relationships.
- More materialistic than spiritual.
- Asthma, diabetes, heart disease.

Raman's Holistic Health Response

- If this is your body type, you need to let go of your innate desire to acquire all things within your grasp. In order to do that, you first need to feel completely secure and contented within yourself. Meditate on the abundance of everything in creation. Recognize there is more out there than you will ever need. Channel the energy within you to feel contented and be in a state of equipoise.

- To control illnesses:
  - Practice yoga/stretching for at least 20 minutes daily.
  - Walk after meals.
  - Avoid fatty, fried foods.
- Juice daily to get essential nutrients, minimizing the desire to snack between meals.

I would like to share one other piece of information with respect to the body types that I have personally benefited from. There are recommended oils for each body type. I would like to list them in this text, although anyone interested in details should get a more comprehensive understanding from a text on the subject.

1. Vata

- Calming oils should be used.
  - Sesame
  - Olive
  - Almond
  - Amla
  - Wheat germ
  - Castor

2. Pitta

- Cooling oils should be used.
  - Coconut
  - Sandalwood
  - Pumpkin seed
  - Almond
  - Sunflower

3. Kapha

- Burning oils should be used.
    - Sesame
    - Safflower
    - Mustard
    - Corn

For a deeper and more accurate understanding on the subject matter in this chapter, you should get one of the numerous books on Ayurvedic Science.

THOUGHT FOR THE DAY

CHANNEL THE ENERGY FOR YOUR BODY TYPE TODAY!

Appendix B

Juice, Fruit and Vegetable Benefits

There are three main tables shown in this chapter.

- Table on Juice Benefits
- Table on Fruit-Vegetable Benefits
- Table on Nutrients

Table 1: Juice Benefits

JUICE	KEY INGREDIENTS	BENEFITS
Morning Energizer	1 small apple	Rich in pectin, which along with the Vitamin C in the apple, helps carry cholesterol out of the body.
	5 medium carrots	Great source of zinc, carotenes, potassium.
	1/2 beet	Beet is great for cleansing the liver.
	1/2-1 inch ginger	Great source of zinc.
	1/2 lemon	Great source of Vitamin C.
Ginger Hopper	1 small apple	Rich in pectin and Vitamin C.
	5 medium carrots	Source of zinc, carotenes, potassium.
	1/2-1 inch ginger	Ginger is anti-inflammatory, also thermogenic — great for weight reduction.

Table 1: Juice Benefits

JUICE	KEY INGREDIENTS	BENEFITS
Ginger Twist	1 small apple	Rich in pectin and Vitamin C.
	5 medium carrots	Source of zinc, carotenes, potassium.
	1 small handful parsley	Parsley is rich in beta carotene and has 3 times Vitamin C of an orange. It has riboflavin (Vitamin B), calcium, iron, magnesium, potassium.
	1/2-1 inch ginger	Great source of zinc.
	1/2 lemon	Source of Vitamin C.
Ginger Waldorf	2 apples	Rich in pectin, which along with the Vitamin C in the apple, helps carry cholesterol out of the body.
	3 celery stalks	Good source of magnesium.
	1/2-1 inch ginger	Great source of zinc.

Table 1: Juice Benefits

JUICE	KEY INGREDIENTS	BENEFITS
Afternoon Refresher	1 cucumber	Cucumbers are diuretics, and great thirst quenchers.
	1/2 lemon	Source of Vitamin C.
Popeye's Power	1 apple	Rich in pectin and Vitamin C.
	1 handful spinach	Reduces risk of cancer, especially of lungs. Most potent in blocking highly carcinogenic nitro-samines.
	5 carrots	Source of zinc, carotenes, potassium.
	1 celery stalk	Good source of magnesium.
	1/2 beet	Good source of calcium and iron.
	1 handful parsley	Rich in Vitamin C, calcium, iron.

Table 1: Juice Benefits

JUICE	KEY INGREDIENTS	BENEFITS
Tomato Delight	2 tomatoes	Twice the anti-oxidant power of beta carotene.
	1 handful spinach	Rich in calcium and iron.
	1 handful basil	Rich in iron, calcium, Vitamin A.
	1/2 lemon	Source of Vitamin C.
Hi-strength Drink	5 carrots	Rich in pectin and Vitamin C.
	2 celery stalks	Contains magnesium — good for strength training.
	1/2 beet	Contains iron — good for strength training.
	2 broccoli pieces	Contains magnesium — good for strength training.
	1/2 lemon	Source of Vitamin C.

Table 1: Juice Benefits

JUICE	KEY INGREDIENTS	BENEFITS
Beauty Drink	1 cucumber	Source of silicon — enhances beauty & diminishes wrinkles. Strengthens bones, skin, hair, fingernails.
	3 carrots	Rich in pectin and Vitamin C.
	1/4 green bell pepper	Source of silicon — enhances beauty & diminishes wrinkles. Strengthens bones, skin, hair, fingernails.
	1/2 lemon	Source of Vitamin C.
Healthy Bones	1 apple	Rich in pectin and Vitamin C.
	1-2 kale leaves	Rich in calcium and Vitamin K (Vitamin K helps calcium absorption in bones), and magnesium (which helps strengthen bones) and boron (reduces calcium excretion).

Table 1: Juice Benefits

JUICE	KEY INGREDIENTS	BENEFITS
	1 handful parsley	Parsley is rich in beta carotene and has 3 times Vitamin C of an orange. It has riboflavin (Vitamin B), calcium, iron, magnesium, potassium.
	5 carrots	Source of zinc, carotenes, potassium.
	1/4 lemon	Source of Vitamin C.
	1/2-1 inch ginger	Great source of zinc.
Energy Builder	3 carrots	Source of zinc, carotenes, potassium.
	1 handful parsley	Parsley helps increase energy.
	1/2-1 inch ginger	Great source of zinc.
	1/4 lemon	Source of Vitamin C.

Table 1: Juice Benefits

JUICE	KEY INGREDIENTS	BENEFITS
Morning Sunrise	1 grapefruit	White inner skin is rich in bioflavonoids — helps to burn excess fat.
	1 orange	High in Vitamin C.
Rise 'n' Shake Smoothie	2 oranges	White inner skin is rich in bioflavonoids; Vitamin C and bioflavonoids together strengthen blood vessels.
	1 banana	Rich in calcium and phosphorus.
	1 mango	Good source of Vitamins C, B1, B2.
	5-6 strawberries	High in manganese and Vitamins C, K.
	Organic apple juice	Source of Vitamin C.

Table 1: Juice Benefits

JUICE	KEY INGREDIENTS	BENEFITS
Morning Express	1 orange	Orange has selenium — powerful antioxidant.
	4-5 carrots	Vitamin C and bioflavonoids (from orange) together strengthen blood vessels.
Beautiful Skin, Hair & Nail Cocktail	1 cucumber	Source of silicon, which strengthens bones, skin, hair and fingernails.
	1/4 green bellpepper	Source of silicon, which strengthens bones, skin, hair and fingernails.
	3 carrots	Source of zinc, carotenes, potassium.
	1/2 lemon	Source of Vitamin C.

Table 1: Juice Benefits

JUICE	KEY INGREDIENTS	BENEFITS
Immune Builder	1 apple	Antiviral properties.
	5 carrots	Source of zinc, carotenes, potassium.
	1 garlic clove	Allicin (in garlic) has antibiotic effect. It is antibacterial, antifungal, antiparasitic, antiviral.
Strawberry Cantaloupe Cocktail	1/2 cantaloupe	Source of carotenoids — cancer-preventive.
	10-12 strawberries	High in manganese and Vitamins C, K.
Santa Fe Salsa Cocktail	1 tomato	Lycopene (in tomato) is powerful antioxidant.
	1/2 cucumber	Good source of silicon.

Table 1: Juice Benefits

JUICE	KEY INGREDIENTS	BENEFITS
	1 bunch cilantro	Good source of Vitamin A.
	1/2 lime	Source of Vitamin C.
Apple Spice	1 apple	Renders viruses inactive.
	1 bunch red grapes	Renders viruses inactive.
	1/2-1 inch ginger	Great source of zinc.
Calcium Cocktail	5 carrots	Source of zinc, carotenes, potassium.
	2-3 kale leaves	High calcium content.
	1 bunch parsley	High calcium content.
	1 apple	Rich in pectin and Vitamin C.
	1/2-1 inch ginger	Great source of zinc.

Table 1: Juice Benefits

JUICE	KEY INGREDIENTS	BENEFITS
Sweet Dreams Nightcap	2 romaine lettuce leaves	Source of calcium, phosphorus.
	3-5 carrots	Source of zinc, carotenes, potassium.
	3 celery stalks	Source of magnesium and calcium (lack of these causes wakefulness).
	1 bunch parsley	Source of magnesium and calcium (lack of these causes wakefulness).
Spinach Cocktail	5 carrots	Source of zinc, carotenes, potassium.
	2-3 kale leaves	High calcium content.
	3-4 spinach leaves	High iron content.
	1 bunch parsley	High calcium content, high iron content.

Table 1: Juice Benefits

JUICE	KEY INGREDIENTS	BENEFITS
	1 apple	Rich in pectin and Vitamin C.
	1/2-1 inch ginger	Great source of zinc.
Triple C	1/4 head cabbage	Cancer preventing property.
	4-5 carrots	Source of zinc, carotenes, potassium.
	3 celery stalks	Source of magnesium and calcium.
Parsley Pep	1 bunch parsley	Energy boost.
	2 celery stalks	Source of magnesium and calcium.
	3-5 carrots	Source of zinc, carotenes, potassium.
	1/2 lemon	Source of Vitamin C.

Table 1: Juice Benefits

JUICE	KEY INGREDIENTS	BENEFITS
Electrolyte Drink	2 oranges	Prevents dehydration.
	4 lemons	Source of Vitamin C.
	2 tablespoons honey	Source of copper, manganese.
	Pinch of salt	
	2 quarts water	

Table 2: Fruit-Vegetable Benefits

Food	*Vitamins*	*Trace Elements*	*Benefits*	*Complementary Foods*
Alfalfa	A, C, K, P	Nitrogen, Potassium, Phosphorus, Calcium, Magnesium, Sulfur, Sodium, Chlorine, Iron, Copper, Manganese, Zinc, Iodine, Selenium, Chromium	Allergies: The mineral salts make blood alkaline, reducing allergic reactions Heart Disease: Removes plaques from arteries.	Combine with carrot juice to prevent intestinal gas. Recipe: 2 tablespoons alfalfa leaves, 5-6 carrots, 1/2 inch ginger.

Table 2: Fruit-Vegetable Benefits

Food	*Vitamins*	*Trace Elements*	*Benefits*	*Complementary Foods*
Apple	A, C, B-Complex	Calcium, Phosphorus, Iron, Sodium, Potassium	Laxative (especially if combined with spinach). Arthritis relief (when fermented). Cholesterol reduction (when juiced with pulp).	Recipe: 5 carrots, 6-8 leaves spinach, handful parsley.
Apricot	A, C	Sulfur, Potassium, Phosphorus, Calcium, Iron	Prevents wrinkles — keeps skin fresh and young. Cancer prevention (due to high Vitamin A). Prevents night blindness & promotes high health (high Vitamin A).	Blend 6-8 apricots with 1 glass of water.

Table 2: Fruit-Vegetable Benefits

Food	*Vitamins*	*Trace Elements*	*Benefits*	*Complementary Foods*
Avocado	A, C, Niacin	Calcium, Phosphorus, Iron, Sodium, Potassium	Prevents rheumatism, arthritis.	Combine 1 avocado with 3-4 tomatoes and 1/2 lemon.
Banana	A, C, Niacin	Calcium, Phosphorus, Iron, Potassium	Heals intestines (when damaged). Cure gastritis and heartburn.	Combine 1 banana with 1 mango and a glass of organic apple juice.

Table 2: Fruit-Vegetable Benefits

Food	*Vitamins*	*Trace Elements*	*Benefits*	*Complementary Foods*
Beet	A, C, B-Complex	Calcium, Phosphorus, Iron, Sodium, Potassium	Prevents/retards cancer.	Combine 1/2 beet with 5 carrots, 1 apple, 1 inch ginger (beet juice by itself is too strong, and the liver may be unable to handle it).

Table 2: Fruit-Vegetable Benefits

Food	*Vitamins*	*Trace Elements*	*Benefits*	*Complementary Foods*
Cab-bage	A, C, B-Complex	Calcium, Phosphorus, Iron, Sodium, Potassium, Sulphur	Cholesterol levels lowered (due to sulphur-containing amino acids), reduced colorectal cancer, diabetes.	Juice cabbage with celery & parsley. CAUTION: Too much cabbage can reduce iodine levels, weakening the thyroid gland.

Table 2: Fruit-Vegetable Benefits

Food	*Vitamins*	*Trace Elements*	*Benefits*	*Complementary Foods*
Canta-loupe	A, C, Niacin	Calcium, Phosphorus, Iron, Sodium, Potassium, Magnesium, Manganese, Copper, Zinc, Cobalt, Chromium	Helps with upset stomach, cooling fevers.	
Carrot	A, C, B-Complex	Calcium, Phosphorus, Iron, Sodium, Potassium, Magnesium, Chromium	Improved vision, complexion.	Juice 5 carrots with 1 apple and 1/2-1 inch ginger.

Table 2: Fruit-Vegetable Benefits

Food	*Vitamins*	*Trace Elements*	*Benefits*	*Complementary Foods*
Celery	A, C, B-Complex	Calcium, Phosphorus, Iron, Sodium, Potassium, Magnesium	Prevents eczema, rash, allergies (strong mineral salts make blood alkaline), blood poisoning (due to rusty nail, dirt in wound), hyperactivity.	Juice 2 celery stalks with 5 carrots, 1 apple and 3/4 inch ginger.
Cherry	A, C, B-Complex	Calcium, Phosphorus, Iron, Sodium, Potassium	Prevents arthritis, acne (blood cleanser), rheumatism; improves skin complexion.	
Bell pepper (green & red)	A, C	Calcium, Phosphorus, Iron, Sodium, Potassium, Magnesium	Aids in weight reduction, pain relief.	Juice with carrots and tomatoes. Add a dash of tobasco sauce.

Table 2: Fruit-Vegetable Benefits

Food	*Vitamins*	*Trace Elements*	*Benefits*	*Complementary Foods*
Citrus juices (grapefruit, lemon, orange, tangerine)	A, C, B-Complex	Calcium, Phosphorus, Iron, Sodium, Potassium, Bioflavonoids in Grapefruit (Hesperidin and Rutin — help burn excess body fat), Boron in Orange, Silicon in Tangerine	Builds immune system, fights congestion and influenza.	

Table 2: Fruit-Vegetable Benefits

Food	*Vitamins*	*Trace Elements*	*Benefits*	*Complementary Foods*
Cucum-ber	A, C, B-Complex	Calcium, Phosphorus, Iron, Sodium, Potassium, Magnesium	Tones skin (cleans toxins from body), prevents dehydration (great for sunburn), soothing when puree applied to insect (bee) stings, poison ivy, poison oak, rash.	Juice 2 cucumbers with 5 carrots and a handful of parsley.

Table 2: Fruit-Vegetable Benefits

Food	*Vitamins*	*Trace Elements*	*Benefits*	*Complementary Foods*
Date, Fig	A, C, Niacin	Calcium, Phosphorus, Iron, Sodium, Potassium	Stimulation for sluggish bowels. Helps with sprue (celiac disease), insomnia, whooping cough, wounds. [Diabetics avoid for constipation — adverse reaction. Due to high sugar content, use with caution for people with high blood sugar, allergies, or yeast infections].	Juice 6 dates, 3 figs, 3 carrots.

Table 2: Fruit-Vegetable Benefits

Food	*Vitamins*	*Trace Elements*	*Benefits*	*Complementary Foods*
Grape, Raisin	A, C, B-Complex	Calcium, Phosphorus, Iron, Sodium, Potassium	Prevents fatigue, heart attack, viral infections.	1 cup of raisins (boil in 3 cups of water, then simmer for 1 hour — strain and freeze), juice 1 pound grapes, 1/2 melon in blender, then add crushed raisin juice.

Table 2: Fruit-Vegetable Benefits

Food	*Vitamins*	*Trace Elements*	*Benefits*	*Complementary Foods*
Kale, Collard	A, C, Niacin	Calcium, Phosphorus, Iron, Sodium, Potassium, Magnesium, Copper, Manganese, Zinc	Prevents osteoporosis. (Due to high calcium, potassium, benefits include blood, heart, skin, muscles, kidneys, nerves; Due to high Vitamin A, strengthen eyes, hair, skin, teeth).	Juice 2 kale leaves, 3 collard leaves, 5 carrots, 1 apple, 1/2-1 inch ginger.

Table 2: Fruit-Vegetable Benefits

Food	*Vitamins*	*Trace Elements*	*Benefits*	*Complementary Foods*
Lettuce	A, C, Niacin	Calcium, Phosphorus, Iron, Sodium, Potassium, Magnesium, Zinc	Lactucarium (in lettuce) has sedative properties and helps in suppressing cough, and aiding insomniacs. Combine with rose petal juice, and apply to temple and forehead for relief from headaches.	Use romaine (3x Vitamin C and 5x Vitamin A than iceberg). Juice 4 leaves with 1/2 bunch parsley, 4 carrots, 1 apple, 1/2-1 inch ginger.
Mango	A, C	Calcium, Phosphorus, Iron, Sodium, Potassium, Magnesium	Helps with hiatal hernia (heartburn), dehydration, blood circulation.	Blend 1 mango with 2 slices papaya, 5 strawberries, 1 banana and 1/2 cup apple juice.

Table 2: Fruit-Vegetable Benefits

Food	*Vitamins*	*Trace Elements*	*Benefits*	*Complementary Foods*
Okra	A, C, Niacin	Calcium, Phosphorus, Iron, Sodium, Potassium, Magnesium, Sulphur (trace amounts of Copper, Manganese and Iodine)	Alternative to blood transfusions (potential blood plasma expander). Helps alleviate joint pain, muscle weakness, and fatigue associated with autoimmune diseases (due to rich protein and trace elements). Relieves gastrointestinal/glandular inflammation (due to unique carbohydrate [sugar]-protein [amino acid] complexes which enter blood plasma and go to sites of inflammation).	Take fresh okra pods and wash them in running water before removing cap and stem end (do not puncture pod). Lightly steam for 3-4 minutes, then blend with the water itself. Add additional water, as needed, to dilute thickness.

Table 2: Fruit-Vegetable Benefits

Food	*Vitamins*	*Trace Elements*	*Benefits*	*Complementary Foods*
Olive	A, C	Calcium, Phosphorus, Iron, Sodium, Potassium	Soften skin.	Juice (with added water). Store in fridge. Rub a little with fingers on cheeks, etc. (DO NOT DRINK — high sodium content)
Papaya	A, C	Calcium, Phosphorus, Iron, Sodium, Potassium, Magnesium	Helps with hiatal hernia (heartburn), improved complexion, liver enlargement	Blend 2 slices papaya with 1 mango, 1 banana, 5 strawberries and 1/2 lime.

Table 2: Fruit-Vegetable Benefits

Food	*Vitamins*	*Trace Elements*	*Benefits*	*Complementary Foods*
Parsley	A, C	Calcium, Phosphorus, Iron, Sodium, Potassium, Magnesium	Helps with allergies, flushing kidneys thereby improving skin.	Juice 1/2 bunch parsley, 5 carrots, 1 apple, 1/2-1 inch ginger.
Passion Fruit	A, C	Calcium, Phosphorus, Iron, Sodium, Potassium, Magnesium	Improves failing eyesight, relief of cystitis (inflammation of urinary bladder), aids insomniacs, cures sore throat.	Peel and remove seeds, then blend or juice the fruit.

Table 2: Fruit-Vegetable Benefits

Food	*Vitamins*	*Trace Elements*	*Benefits*	*Complementary Foods*
Peach, Pear	A, C (Niacin in peach)	Calcium, Phosphorus, Iron, Sodium, Potassium, Magnesium	Tonic for the lungs, fevers, indigestion, morning or moticn sickness.	Cut 1 unpeeled peach and remove pit. Blend with 1 unpeeled pear and 1 cup of water. Drink at room temperature (chilled juice will harm already injured lungs).

Table 2: Fruit-Vegetable Benefits

Food	*Vitamins*	*Trace Elements*	*Benefits*	*Complementary Foods*
Pea	A, C, Niacin	Calcium, Phosphorus, Iron, Sodium, Potassium, Magnesium	Helps dissolve blood clots, alleviates problems with celiac disease (sprue or gluten-sensitive enteropathy), and helps Irritable Bowel Syndrome (IBS — painful distended abdomen and spells of diarrhea and constipation).	Blend a cup of shelled peas till it is liquid. (For IBS, heat it with powdered cardamom and ground ginger root — and serve warm).

Table 2: Fruit-Vegetable Benefits

Food	*Vitamins*	*Trace Elements*	*Benefits*	*Complementary Foods*
Plums	A, C	Calcium, Phosphorus, Iron, Sodium, Potassium, Magnesium	Alleviates gastritis, hyperacidity (high amounts of potassium and magnesium squeeze water from the colon and drop into the GI tract, providing relief).	Remove pits from 1 cup of plums and blend at high speed.

Table 2: Fruit-Vegetable Benefits

Food	*Vitamins*	*Trace Elements*	*Benefits*	*Complementary Foods*
Pump-kin	A, C, Niacin (extreme-ly high Vitamin A content)	Calcium, Phosphorus, Iron, Sodium, Potassium, Magnesium	Helps allergies, skin problems, vision disorders, blood sugar imbalances, infections, joint swelling, lung problems, elevated cholesterol and triglyceride levels, liver disturbances. (Zuni and Hopi Indians used this with some success to treat leukemia).	Remove peel and seeds. Then juice 1/4 pumpkin with carrots to improve taste. (Drink 1-2 glasses — NOT more than 2 due to high Vitamin A content).

Table 2: Fruit-Vegetable Benefits

Food	*Vitamins*	*Trace Elements*	*Benefits*	*Complementary Foods*
Radish	A, C	Calcium, Phosphorus, Iron, Sodium, Potassium, Magnesium, Selenium, Zinc (facilitates cell production, repair of damaged tissues, and normal cell growth)	Treatment for hypothyroidism (producing too little thyroxine) and hyperthyroidism (too much thyroxine — also called Graves disease), constipation, fatty liver disease (enlarged due to diabetes), gallbladder inflammation.	Juice 1 bunch radishes with 3-5 carrots. (Radish juice is too strong in its reaction to be taken alone).

Table 2: Fruit-Vegetable Benefits

Food	*Vitamins*	*Trace Elements*	*Benefits*	*Complementary Foods*
Rhu-barb	A, C, Folic acid	Calcium, Phosphorus, Iron, Sodium, Potassium, Magnesium	Treatment for gum disease (gingivitis), tartar and plaque build-up (Use juice to brush teeth — DO NOT SWALLOW).	Hard to juice (contains oxalic acid — not good for the body if swallowed frequently).
Spinach	A, C, Biotin, E	Calcium, Phosphorus, Iron, Sodium, Potassium, Magnesium, Manganese, Zinc	Alleviates anemia, fatigue.	Juice 1 bunch spinach with 3 carrots and 2 tomatoes.

Table 2: Fruit-Vegetable Benefits

Food	*Vitamins*	*Trace Elements*	*Benefits*	*Complementary Foods*
String Beans	A, C, Folic acid	Calcium, Phosphorus, Iron, Sodium, Potassium, Magnesium	Alleviates diabetes, hypoglycemia (resuscitates the pancreas, spleen, and liver). Take 3-5 times a day.	Juice a handful of beans with 2-3 carrots. Add a little water, if needed.
Tomato	A, C, Folic acid, Biotin	Calcium, Phosphorus, Iron, Sodium, Potassium, Magnesium	Improves liver functioning, alleviates chronic fatigue syndrome, fatigue; helps with hypoglycemia; creates appetite.	Juice or blend, then add a little lime or lemon juice with a dash of pepper.

Table 2: Fruit-Vegetable Benefits

Food	*Vitamins*	*Trace Elements*	*Benefits*	*Complementary Foods*
Water-melon	A, C, Folic acid	Calcium, Phosphorus, Iron, Sodium, Potassium, Magnesium, Zinc	Aid recovery from illness, arthritis & gout (flushes uric acid from system), skin problems (flushes a lot of the acids from the system and renews the blood).	Juice 3-4 slices, and strain to remove seeds. Or blend the seedless variety.

Table 2: Fruit-Vegetable Benefits

Food	*Vitamins*	*Trace Elements*	*Benefits*	*Complementary Foods*
Wheatgrass, Barleygrass	A, K, C, E, Thiamin, Choline, Riboflavin, Pyridoxine, B-12, Niacin, Pantothenic acid, Biotin, Folic acid	Calcium, Phosphorus, Iron, Sodium, Potassium, Magnesium, Manganese, Zinc, Iodine, Selenium, Copper, Cobalt	GIVES LIFE, alleviates fatigue (rich in vitamins, minerals and enzymes), infections (high Vitamin A, C enhance liver function), malnutrition.	Juice a cup of wheatgrass with 1/2 beet, and 3-5 carrots. (Alternately, use 1 tablespoon of Kyo-Green and blend with juice made from 5 carrots, 1 apple, 1/4 beet, 1/2 inch ginger).

Table 2: Fruit-Vegetable Benefits

Food	*Vitamins*	*Trace Elements*	*Benefits*	*Complementary Foods*
Zucchini, Squash	A, C, Niacin	Calcium, Phosphorus, Iron, Sodium, Potassium, Magnesium	Helps with chronic fatigue syndrome, calcium mal-absorption, osteoporosis, fractures, bone breaks (Calcium, phosphorus, magnesium, sodium present in about equal amounts. With strong potassium, able to mend sooner than with individual food supplements).	Juice 1/4 zucchini with 3-4 carrots, 1 tomato. (Drink 1 cup with each meal)

Table 3: Nutrient Chart

Vitamin A	*Vitamin B1*	*Vitamin B2*	*Vitamin B3*	*Vitamin B5*
Carrots	Nuts	Green vegetables	Green vegetables	Potatoes
Broccoli	Seeds	Beans	Beans	Egg yolks
Tomatoes	Legumes	Cheese	Rice	Orange juice
Yellow squash	Wheat germ	Milk	Bran	Brewer's yeast
Spinach	Poultry	Egg yolks	Whole wheat	Legumes
Apricots	Fish	Nuts, Whole grains	Nuts	Whole grains
Peaches	Brown rice	Yogurt	Brewer's yeast	Mushrooms

Table 3: Nutrient Chart

Vitamin A	*Vitamin B1*	*Vitamin B2*	*Vitamin B3*	*Vitamin B5*
Kale	Egg yolks	Poultry	Fish	Salmon
Eggs	Whole grains	Green vegetables	Dairy	Wheat germ
Fish liver oil	Brewer's yeast		Poultry	
Dairy	Seafood		Eggs	
	Potatoes		Peas	

Table 4: Nutrient Chart (contd)

Vitamin B6	*Vitamin B9*	*Vitamin B12*	*Vitamin C*	*Vitamin D*
Fruits (bananas)	Root vegetables	Broccoli	Citrus fruits	Fish oils
Nuts	Tuna	Dairy	Cantaloupe	Mushrooms
Seeds	Dairy	Eggs	Broccoli	Herring
Milk	Oysters	Fish	Tomatoes	Sardines
Cabbage	Salmon	Cereals	Mangos	Egg yolks
Cantaloupe	Leafy green veggies		Sprouted alfalfa	
Legumes	Brewer's yeast		Seeds	Tuna
Peas	Whole grains		Peppers	
Wheat germ	Wheat germ		Papaya	

Table 4: Nutrient Chart (contd)

Vitamin B6	*Vitamin B9*	*Vitamin B12*	*Vitamin C*	*Vitamin D*
Whole grains			Strawberries	
Brown rice			Potatoes	
Prunes			Chilies	
Fish				
Leafy greens				
Brewer's yeast				
Soybeans				

Table 5: Nutrient Chart (contd)

Vitamin E	*Vitamin H*	*Vitamin K*	*Calcium*	*Choline*
Nuts	Sardines	Leafy green vegetables	Beans	Leafy green vegetables
Seeds	Legumes	Cauliflower	Fruits	Egg yolks
Spinach	Egg yolks	Brussels sprouts	Spinach	Brewer's yeast
Brussels sprouts	Lentils	Tomatoes	Green vegetables	Fish
Soybeans	Whole grains	Broccoli		Legumes
Cold pressed oils	Brewer's yeast	Soybeans		Soybeans
Whole wheat	Oats	Alfalfa		Wheat germ
Sweet potatoes	Nuts	Fish liver oils		

Table 5: Nutrient Chart (contd)

Vitamin E	*Vitamin H*	*Vitamin K*	*Calcium*	*Choline*
Wheat germ	Wheat germ	Egg yolks		
Dark green vegetables				
Eggs				
Oatmeal				

THOUGHT FOR THE DAY

ENERGIZE YOUR IMMUNE SYSTEM WITH LIVE FOODS!

Appendix C

Meditative Reflections

Listed below are a few thoughts that help keep the mind centered and enable the build-up of your energy source.

Personal

1. **I am grateful for my family to share life's experiences with.**

2. **I am grateful for my friends and their support.**

3. **I am grateful for my health so I can appreciate life.**

4. **I am grateful for my vision so I can see the beauty around me.**

5. **I am grateful for my hands that enable me to work easily.**

6. **I am grateful for my legs that let me travel and see the world.**

7. **I am grateful for my hearing so I can listen to the voices of loved ones.**

8. **I am grateful for my house that affords me shelter.**

9. **I am grateful for the food that helps nourish me.**

10. **I am grateful for this opportunity to channel my energy.**

Creation

I am grateful for these eyes so I can see:

1. **The beauty in the flowers,**

2. **The colors of the rainbow,**

3. **The magnificent sunrise,**

4. **The changing seasons,**

5. **The soaring eagle,**

6. **The multi-colored butterflies,**
7. **The majestic mountains.**

I am grateful for these ears so I can hear:

1. **The laughter of the children,**
2. **The chirping of the cricket,**
3. **The heart-rending cries of the pied-cuckoo,**
4. **The babbling of the brook,**
5. **The rustling of the leaves,**
6. **The sound of the waves crashing on the beach,**
7. **The crackling of the firewood.**

I am grateful for this opportunity to experience Life!